D0120201

A CELEBRATION OF THE LIGHT

A Celebration
of the Light

Zen in the Novels of
Neil Gunn

John Burns

CANONGATE

First published in Great Britain in 1988
by Canongate Publishing Ltd., 17 Jeffrey Street, Edinburgh.

First published in the United States of America in 1988
by Barnes and Noble Books.

The publishers acknowledge the financial
assistance of the Scottish Arts Council in the
publication of this volume.

British Library Cataloguing in Publication Data.

Burns, John
A celebration of the light: Zen in the novels of Neil Gunn.
1. Fiction in English. Gunn, Neil M. (Neil Miller), 1891–1973.
Influence of Zen Buddhism.
I. Title 823'.912.

ISBN 0–86241–109–2

Typeset by Buccleuch Printers Ltd., Hawick.
Printed and bound in Great Britain by Billings & Sons Ltd.

For
Vivien

it is all
a celebration of the light

W. C. WILLIAMS

ACKNOWLEDGEMENTS & AUTHOR'S NOTE

Although the Romanizing of Chinese and Japanese has been systematized, no one system has been adopted as standard by publishers around the world. As a result, in quoting faithfully from a wide variety of published sources by authors and translators of Zen and Tao writings, it is inevitable that inconsistencies in spelling, capitalization and hyphenation occur within the text.

Within each chapter, unattributed quotes with page reference numbers only refer to the first edition of the Gunn novel under discussion in that chapter (see Contents List and Bibliography).

The title, 'Celebration of the Light', comes from a poem, 'Asphodel, That Greeny Flower' by William Carlos Williams in Pictures of Breughel and Other Poems (see Bibliography).

Thanks are due to: the staff of Edinburgh Public Libraries and Edinburgh University Library; to the staff of the National Library of Scotland and to Mr Stanley Simpson, Assistant Keeper in the Department of Manuscripts in that Library; to Mr Dairmid Gunn for granting me access to Neil Gunn's papers and for permission to quote from them and from the novels referred to in this book; to Ann MacSween, who typed the original manuscript; to Colin Nicholson, George Bruce, Alex Reid, Stewart Conn, and F. R. Hart with whom I discussed various aspects of Neil Gunn's life and art; to Alan Spence, William Dolby and J. B. Pick who offered valuable criticism at various stages in the preparation of the manuscript.

Finally, I would like to extend a special word of thanks to Ian Campbell for his guidance and his infinite patience while I was working on the thesis on which this book is based; and to Sarah Mackie for her unfailing helpfulness and clear vision in preparing the manuscript for publication.

John Burns

CONTENTS

FOREWORD

The Burns thesis is the most enlightening and suggestive discussion I have read of Neil's books in some years. I learned something on every page. It is precisely the sort of treatment that should prove most interesting and illuminating to foreign readers (especially Americans), for whom the universal psychological and spiritual substance of Neil's books must prove important.

The argument of the book is wonderfully careful, and it commands the entire discussion. Burns assiduously AVOIDS making Neil Gunn into a Zen philosopher, and carefully avoids any silly suggestion that Neil was 'influenced' in some mechanical way. He simply shows as he says that Zen and Taoist psychology provides the best 'philosophical model' for understanding the essentials of experience in all of Neil's books. The particulars of experience in the book are interpreted with an admirably empirical (that is UNdogmatic, sound, perceptive) air. The relevant analogies in Zen and Taoism are beautifully interwoven, so that the thought NEVER seems forced, and there is no hint of thesis-grinding.

I was also exicted by the revelation of underlying unity in the books from the earliest to the final Saltire articles; I have never seen this done so well before. And it simply invalidates all of the clichéd divisions normally imposed on Neil's development. To do this, Burns needed a sample of novels drawn from various parts or stages, and I think his sample is both fair and sound. The way Burns has juxtaposed elements from such

xi

seemingly different books revealed things to me I had never been able to work out before, e.g. the real importance of dark Mairi; the final struggles of Finn in *The Silver Darlings*; the meaning of *The Serpent*. My reading will never be the same again after reading Burns.

F. R. Hart
Hingham, Mass.
4 July 1987

LIGHT, DELIGHT AND ZEN
Introduction

Near the end of his life Neil Gunn was delighted to come across
a Japanese philosopher's statement that 'the real nature of
man's mind is delight'[1] because it echoed exactly the spirit that
informed his own work. For the central impulse of his fiction is
the continual exploration of those brief moments of insight that
'irradiate life with delight'. All of Gunn's novels are concerned
with this quest, but as he grew older this exploration of the light
and delight at life's core became increasingly important to him
both as a man and as a writer. In *The Lost Chart* Joe, the artist,
says, 'The darkness creates drama ready-made for man; but
man has to create his own drama of the light' (p.178) and in its
continual impulse to go beyond darkness and despair, to chart
the changes and subtleties of life's positive and creative aspects,
Gunn's fiction is very clearly just such a drama of the light.

But the wisdom that informed such a vision did not come
easily. The early novels, particularly *The Grey Coast* and *The Lost
Glen*, are bitter and angry. *The Grey Coast* presents a grim picture
of the economic realities of living in Caithness at the turn of the
century, while *The Lost Glen* is torn apart by the intensity of its
author's questioning. Yet despite the difficulties, the false
starts, the uncertainties of beginning to write, Gunn gradually
evolved a more creative response to life. Among these early
novels *Morning Tide*, with its optimism and hope, its sense of
the breaking of a new dawn, stands out. But even in those other
dark, early novels there are gleams of light: gleams of light that
Gunn would gradually develop into a subtle and marvellous art.

1

His novels present a comprehensive vision of Highland history from the ninth century (*Sun Circle*) through the devastation of the Clearances (*Butcher's Broom*) into the period of economic prosperity which came with the rise of the herring fishing industry in the early nineteenth century (*The Silver Darlings*), and then to the economic depression of our own century following the decline of that same fishing industry (*The Grey Coast, The Lost Glen*). In itself this is a remarkable achievement, yet this is only the surface of Gunn's world. However much his writing reflects the social and historical reality of life in the Highlands, its real impact is more universal, being concerned with each man's individual struggle towards wholeness and integration.

Neil Gunn's intuitive awareness of the wholeness and integration of the world grew naturally out of the community in which he grew up. In *Highland River* he writes:

> The son did not love the mother more than the father, but loved each differently in her sphere or his. And the affection, being disciplined and delicate, became part of all the ways of life . . . It went about with them everywhere, because everywhere they went had something to do with the communal life, the centre of which was the home. Ultimately the shieling meant food, the river fish, and the peat-bank fire. The contacts were direct and the results were seen. There was thus about the most ordinary labour some of the excitement of creation. Nor could cold or gloom or hunger or other discomfort completely obscure the sense of family unity in its life struggle; on the contrary, as with all creative effort, the discomforts, and setbacks, particularly in retrospect, add some extra quality of fineness or delight. (p.105)

Here personal and communal identity is felt as a potent mystery, graspable only through the ordinary details of every-day life—'the contacts were direct and the results were seen'— but filled always with an awareness of another, more extra-ordinary reality just beyond the mind's grasp.

For Gunn, awareness of this other, more extraordinary dimension comes in brief moments of insight and reconcilia-tion. In his autobiography he calls such moments 'atoms of delight', and suggests that only through recognising the significance of such moments can a man attain to wisdom and learn to hold the darkness at bay. The 'atom' is that elusive moment of heightened awareness in which life is experienced as a realm of wonder and delight.

This quality of awareness illuminates all of Neil Gunn's fiction where it is often symbolised by light itself, his central image of complete awareness being that of a world literally filled with light as described in *Highland Pack*:

> The sun would pierce through, and all the world would fill with light; brim and tremble and spill over, and off sped the light over the grass and in among the wild roses and glittering across the sea. The sheer freshness of such a moment had surely the spirit of creation in it, a first creation. (p.157)

This vision of a world of light became the still point around which Gunn's fiction coheres; all of his many other interests—historical, sociological, psychological, and political—find their common centre here. This is the 'message' of his autobiographical work, *The Atom of Delight*, a book published at the end of his writing career giving the author's view of his subjects and techniques. If the reader can grasp his overriding vision of the world as a creative process, then everything else in the novels falls into place.

At the heart of Gunn's vision lies a profound awareness of the interrelatedness of all life. And whereas much modern literature is bleak and pessimistic, stressing the alienation of the individual both from society and from his own essential nature, Gunn's fiction conveys a real sense of integration and whole-ness—the quality which he referred to as *delight*. His books are filled with this sense of delight—an intense awareness of the living variety of the world, and of man's involvement in it. The boy, Kenn, in *Highland River* goes down to the village harbour and there encounters life in all its vibrant movement and colour:

> All the life of that little Highland world met where the river met the sea. When the harbour swung to high tide and the boats came in with their shots of herring, human activity brimmed over as the herrings over the cran basket when the two men on the halyard rope, faces to the sky, pulled fist over fist, in heaving rhythm.

3

> Limber men, blue-jerseyed, with lean belly muscles and slender
> hips, quick-footed as dancers. And great dancers they were. They
> could dance in the leather sea-boots that came to their thighs, or
> sway drunken in a public house on rooted feet . . . It was a world
> of action, of doing. It had the warmth of colour in faces and of
> flashing eyes. One could rush to it with excitement. (p.67)

And in *The Well at the World's End*, Peter Munro, in his quest for
Enlightenment, has this remarkable vision of the world:

> As he followed the slanting path the bushes came together into a
> low sheltering wood that had looked from a distance like a
> coverlet on the hillside. Stunted birch trees and hazels full of small
> singing or chirping birds: chaffinches, tits, green linnets, a
> scolding blackbird, a resounding robin; a flash, a flight, a scurry;
> with bounteous green-leaved space for one and all. Looking upon
> this ardent coloured world he forgot himself and thought of
> nothing, so his eye had time for an extra clarity of vision, an
> unusual capacity to perceive and to distinguish. It was delightful,
> forever shading off into the subtle and the rare, delight behind
> delight in an objectivity external as the birdnotes and almost as
> clear; beyond him, like the fragrant air he breathed. (p.102)

This kind of writing is rare; it brings together abstract and
concrete, and conveys a real sense of the world as a living
organism in which man is intimately involved. It not only
describes, but also awakens in the reader that 'extra clarity of
vision' which goes beyong logic, and is a direct apprehension of
the world and of man's place in it. This is a way of seeing that
has much in common with such Eastern ways of thought as Zen
Buddhism and Taoism which, with their faith in the spontaneous functioning of the unconscious mind, have recently
generated a great deal of interest in the West. It is, therefore,
not surprising that Neil Gunn acknowledged this connection
and in his later years devoted much time to exploring it.

F. R. Hart and J. B. Pick date the beginning of Gunn's explicit
interest in Zen precisely: 1953.[2] In that year Pick sent him a
copy of Eugen Herrigel's *Zen in the Art of Archery*, after its
publication in English. The fact that Gunn devoted a central
chapter of *The Atom of Delight* to an account of this book attests
to its importance for him. We know also, from notebooks in the

4

National Library of Scotland, that he read and took notes from translations and commentaries such as the Richard Wilhelm/ C. G. Jung edition of *The Secret of the Golden Flower*, John Blofeld's translation of *The Zen Teaching of Huang Po*, and D. T. Suzuki's *The Zen Doctrine of No Mind*. Other sources reveal his familiarity with Suzuki's *Essays In Zen Buddhism*, Alan Watts' *The Way of Zen*, Hubert Benoit's *The Supreme Doctrine*, Paul Reps' *Zen Flesh, Zen Bones*, Herrigel's *The Method of Zen* and Nancy Wilson Ross's 'delightful anthology', *The World of Zen*,[3] a book about which he wrote with tongue in cheek to Professor Hart, revealing something of his delighted acceptance of Zen's illogicality:

> . . . have a look at it, when you feel like being irresponsible. It covers the whole realm, with sufficient intellectual passages— essays—to keep you going from one nothing to the next. Don't mention it to the Zen 'authorities' about—enjoy it in silence. When you find yourself escaping to it for fun you're on the way.[4]

J. B. Pick recalls that Gunn was 'deeply impressed' by Herrigel's *The Method of Zen*, and that in *Zen Flesh, Zen Bones*, a book Gunn kept by his bedside in his later years, 'he was particularly taken with the humour of the Ch'an (Zen) masters', and that he was 'delighted' by the section in that book which featured '112 ways to open the invisible door of consciousness'.[5]

The picture that emerges is of a man who perceived something of the parallels between his own work and an apparently alien tradition, and who was sufficiently impressed by these parallels to investigate the matter seriously, even to the extent of using this knowledge of Eastern ways of liberation to dictate the structure of his autobiography. In general, though, it is pointless to pore over Gunn's novels seeking out allusions or quotations which might seem to give solid proof of any 'influence' Zen might have had on his thought and on his art as a novelist. Rather, what is revealed in his writings is an extraordinary similarity of temperament between the Scottish writer and certain Far Eastern philosophers. This is the way in which Gunn himself regarded the matter, as he explained in a letter to Professor Hart while discussing the writing of *The Green Isle of the Great Deep*:

5

Anyway, you may take it that if I got interested in the 'East', as we may call it, it was not for lack of knowledge of the West's more hellishly abstractive subtleties. But when you ask me to tell you about this 'East', I just don't know how to begin—or even what to say, for the use of paradox can be irritating. However, I can say this, that when I began reading about Zen, I seemed to know a lot about it and to have used it in my writings from the beginning![6]

And a letter to Professor Nakamura makes the same point:

With such work when I came to read it I always felt immediately at home, even familiarly, because really, I suppose, any ideas I may have expressed concerning such notions as a 'second self' came from personal experience, including flashes of insight or intuition, and not, primarily anyhow, from ideas and theories which have been got from others. Often when such ideas or theories coincide more or less with notions of his own the writer will happily find them acceptable; they may even help to clarify his mind; anyway he is always delighted to meet them for they are companionable.[7]

Nowhere does Gunn claim to have authoritative knowledge of Zen, or of any other Eastern philosophy: 'it is far from my intention or ability even to suggest the scope of Zen or what living by Zen means.'[8] All he claims is that his own mind is at home in exploring the same psychological territory. This is the underlying assumption of a series of articles published in Alexander Reid's *Saltire Review*[9] in which Gunn connects Zen with his own experiences of living in the Highlands. In encountering Zen, Neil Gunn recognised a tradition that had for centuries explored a region remarkably similar to that which he had explored in his novels. As Professor Hart put it, Gunn's encounter with Eastern philosophy 'was less the discovery of something new than the delighted recognition, in a remote place, of something he had known and sought to convey all along'.[10]

This idea of recognition has also been stressed by J. B. Pick, both in published work and in unpublished correspondence. His essay 'The Boy in the Stream'[11] shows how one particular incident, related in *The Atom of Delight*, is of central importance to the nature of Gunn's art. In a letter to the present writer Mr Pick emphasised that Gunn did not need to read books to understand the Zen experience. What Herrigel told him, he recognised as something which he had long known and practised. Zen did not 'influence' him: it simply became another illustration of what he understood about the nature of man and life: 'He meditated, expanded, mythologised his own experiences and recognised a variety of strands of thought from what is usually called "the East" which he felt confirmed those experiences.'[12]

Gunn's own account of this delighted recognition of a path similar to his own is given in *The Atom of Delight*, and in the *Saltire Review* articles, while ten years later two related articles appeared in Pick's periodical *Point* which take up the same theme and thus attest to his continuing interest in the subject.

What Gunn recognised and responded to in Zen Buddhism was a way of thought that recognised the role of the irrational in man's life. Zen deals not in explanations and concepts but rather in direct apprehension of the reality, or what Buddhists call the 'suchness' of the world. Insight of this kind comes in brief flashes of inspiration which Zen Buddhists call *satori*, and in these moments man is able to comprehend his relation to the world and can see the flaws in his habitual 'idea' of what this relation is. In his early novel *Morning Tide* Neil Gunn wrote: 'For truth is not of words, but of vision. Thus many things that are spoken contradict one another, but in the vision there is no contradiction.' (p.272) Throughout his novels different characters are brought to moments of vision in which the validity of this statement is brought home to them.

For Gunn there are two worlds; the world we see every day, and the world which lies beyond this, the other landscape of delight. Man truly belongs on the other landscape but is tied to the mundane world by habit and fear. Nevertheless, all events of significance take place on the other landscape and man is sometimes able to glimpse the lineaments of that landscape before fear and habit once again take over his perception and he retreats into the protective shell of his ego. But the other landscape is the 'real' world, and whether or not man wants to face it he is driven by the intensity of those glimpses to explore this landscape more fully, until in the end the protective shell of

7

the ego is broken and he is liberated, able to see the world as a realm of delight.

In the novels such moments of awareness often come unasked, as they do in life. In the article 'Light' in Pick's magazine *Point*, Gunn describes the attempt to understand such moments consciously, and the growing realisation that the conscious mind is not enough:

> But it's the next and final step that's the difficult one—and really quite impossible to describe because of its unique nature . . . In the end thought itself gets choked and the mind becomes a void. It's at this point that the miracle happens, and the void, the void itself, gets lit up: the light spreads, burgeons; it is suffused with wonder, delight, a miraculous sense of freedom.[13]

And in his last novel, *The Other Landscape*, Gunn hints that a similar mode of apprehension is at work in our response to a work of art:

> But there was something more, and that was, in a word, the sudden insight. It always came suddenly. The mist, the verbiage, cleared and lo! there was what had not been seen. The true work of art produces the sense of surprise, delight, but the great work also produces something more. What had been unthinkable is in a moment apprehended. (p.306)

This is where Gunn connects directly with Zen, for what he is describing is nothing less than the Zen concept of *satori*, the intuitive flash of insight into reality. It was Gunn's own awareness of the significance of such moments—his atoms of delight—that allowed him to respond so positively to Zen.

Historically, Zen is a particular form of Buddhism with its own rituals and traditions which arose in China in the sixth century as a result of the interplay between Indian Mahāyāna Buddhism and native Chinese Taoism. In the twelfth century Zen was introduced to Japan, from where in the twentieth century it has come to the West. But this is only its outward aspect. The inner reality of Zen is timeless and universal.

This inner reality can only be penetrated as a result of intense personal effort, and it is this hidden internal reality that makes Zen, according to Chang Chen-chi, 'the most difficult, puzzling, and complicated subject in the field of Buddhist study'.[14] This is particularly so for the Westerner, because as Watts has emphasised, Zen does not fit readily into any of the formal categories of modern Western thought. Zen is what is known in the East as a 'way of liberation', and as such it is concerned not with the propagation of any particular set of beliefs or dogma, but with the attainment of a direct, intuitive grasp of reality:

> Outside teaching; apart from tradition.
> Not founded on words and letters
> Pointing directly to the human mind.
> Seeing into one's nature and attaining Buddhahood.[15]

To its adherents, Zen is the very essence of Buddhism because of its deep concern to realise the Buddha's Enlightenment as an actuality, and not merely as an intellectual concept.

Before Buddhism arrived in China, this love of simplicity and directness had been nurtured by the native tradition of Taoism. Taoism was fertile ground for the growth and development of Zen because of its insistence that the ultimate reality, or *Tao*, can never be adequately described or even imagined, and that its reality can only be apprehended by a non-logical awareness. This is stressed again and again in the principal text of Taoism, Lao Tsu's *Tao Te Ching* whose central message is that 'The Tao that can be explained is not the true Tao'. And the constant awareness of the ungraspable nature of the ultimate reality is, for the Taoist, the beginning of an attitude of profound reverence before the vast mystery of creation.

For the Taoist the world is not a collection of separate objects or things, but is a continually changing process which becomes manifest in the interaction of the opposite but complementary forces *yin* and *yang*. For the Chinese the world is not a war between positive and negative forces, but a process in which both positive and negative have equal relevance. Tao is indefinable, but it is so precisely because while seeking to define it man is inescapably still part of it. And it is because of this inseparability of man and environment that the philosophy of Taoism is really, like that of Zen, a practical process of learning how to live in accordance with universal principles.

The end of Zen, as of Taoism, is just to be simply and naturally human, not to experience some wondrous vision, nor to acquire superhuman powers. It is rather the surprised wonder at realising that one had possessed the object of the search all along. It is this sense of wonder and delight that irradiates Neil Gunn's favourite Zen poem, P'ang-yun's:

> I fetch water. I break sticks. Miracles happen!

This experience of *satori* or Enlightenment is felt as liberating and expansive as one is freed from the illusions which formerly cramped and restricted, an experience Gunn describes in *The Well at the World's End*: 'once you pushed through the boundaries of personal importance things opened out; a wider range of freedom.' (p.263) One of the most vivid descriptions of this feeling is the Taoist Lieh-tzu's 'riding on the wind':

> I was wholly unconscious of what my body was resting on, or what was under my feet. I was borne this way and that on the wind, like dry chaff or leaves falling from a tree. In fact, I knew not whether the wind was riding on me or I on the wind.[16]

Other texts, such as the *T'ai I Chin Hua Tsung Chi* (*The Secret of the Golden Flower*) which Gunn knew, use the image of the 'circulation of the light' to describe the psychic process of awakening. And we find a similar concentration on light and lightness in the world of Neil Gunn's fiction where it can be seen either in the way in which many of his central characters see the world, or in the lightness and delicacy of Gunn's own treatment of his themes. This lightness of touch is perhaps best seen in books like *Morning Tide* or *Young Art and Old Hector* where he is able to evoke all the complex emotions of childhood and adolescence with no trace of sentimentality. This is where Gunn, like Zen itself, is deceptively simple: but the lightness and clarity of his vision is not an evasion of life's very real problems, rather it is the result of having lived through such problems and learning how to deal with them.

Although the renewed vision of Enlightenment, of *satori*, goes beyond many of our normal categories of logic it is certainly not vague or unintelligible. Rather it is of perfect simplicity, giving an extra clarity of vision. This is due to the stripping away of illusion so that man sees the world more clearly. The dualistic process of rational thought will never 'see' in this way, as it constantly upholds the illusion that man exists in some way separate from the world he thinks about. Thinking in this way there is always a split between 'the thinker' and that which is 'thought' about. Lancelot Whyte points out in *The Next Development in Man*, that thought of this kind only begins when action is blocked:

> Thought is born of failure. When action satisfies there is no residue to hold the attention; to think is to confess a lack of adjustment which we must stop to consider. Only when the human organism fails to achieve an adequate response to its situation is there material for the processes of thought, and the greater the failure the more searching they become . . .[17]

Life lived beyond thought has a different 'feel' to it, a different flavour, the kind of detached joy experienced when any action, however small, is performed perfectly, and all one's energy is focussed in that action rather than being diffused into all the millions of trivial worries and distractions which for most of us make up the thinking process. This is not to act unthinkingly; rather it is to think and act wholeheartedly, using one's energy with much greater precision than is usual. The way beyond limited attention to this state of delight in one's activity is through the exercise of a more intuitive kind of understanding, which Buddhists call *prajñā*, and which is learned through the discipline of meditation, a word which in the West is capable of many distortions of meaning, but which must be central to any discussion of Zen.

Of all the schools of Buddhism Zen is the most thorough-going in its insistence on the importance of meditation. The word *Zen* itself is the Japanese form of the Chinese *Ch'an*, which is in turn a translation of an Indian term *dhyāna* meaning 'meditation'. Meditation is therefore inextricably bound up with the Zen life. But although Zen training does involve long periods of formal sitting meditation or *zāzen*, the aim of Zen is something more dynamic than the word 'meditation' might suggest to us in the West.

11

There is no mystery in meditation. It is simply a way of learning to use a more intuitive approach to living so as to get rid of that self-consciousness that so often prevents us from acting freely. The practice of meditation is the development of what Shunryu Suzuki calls 'Zen Mind, Beginner's Mind'—an openness and responsiveness to every possibility which can arise so that there is no hesitation, no lack of adjustment to circumstances. The 'beginner' can do this because, ideally, his mind is free and uncluttered, ready to learn. As knowledge grows it easily becomes formalised and can begin to destroy one's original spontaneity: 'In the beginner's mind there are many possibilities, but in the expert's there are few.'[18]

'Beginner's mind' is not mere mindlessness. It is a state of mind which is quietly attentive, always ready to respond to the ever-changing circumstances of life. We all know the double-bind of being unable to do something because we are trying too hard, constantly reminding ourselves of the need to concentrate, rather than just *doing* it. Meditation is a way of handling this kind of situation. One learns how to act spontaneously simply by acting spontaneously.

The greatest obstacle to the development of the meditative mind is man's ego, the constant assumption that 'I' am doing 'this', that 'I' am separate from the rest of the world and thus do things *to* it rather than functioning as an integral part of a larger process. This dualistic way of thinking has long been the characteristic mode of thought in the West. The East, on the other hand, has always recognised the inseparability of man and universe. The Great Triad of Taoism sees man as the point of intersection of Heaven and Earth, so demonstrating his intimate relationship with an ordered cosmos. And the same idea of the interrelationship of man and his world underlies the Tantric schools of both Hinduism and Buddhism.

> You yourself are the eternal energy which appears as this universe. You didn't come into this world, you came out of it, like a wave from the ocean, you are not a stranger here. On the contrary, everything that happens to you, everything that you experience, is your *karma*: your own doing. This, though expressed in differing ways, is the central philosophy of both Hinduism and Buddhism, cradled alike in the culture of ancient India.[19]

In Zen itself there are two main ways of coming to this realisation, and these two methods of meditation are among the distinguishing characteristics of the two major schools of Zen as they survive today. Rinzai Zen favours the *koan* method of instruction in which the student is given a *koan* or problem by the Master and has to engage all his energy in attempting to solve this problem. It is generally a question based on a remark made by a former Zen master. The *koan* is designed so as to be incapable of logical solution, and is a controlled and calculated attempt to drive the student beyond logic to the intuitive wisdom of *prajñā*. The Soto school, on the other hand, regards this practice as misleading and places more emphasis on 'quiet sitting', using *zāzen* as a way of stilling the persistent chatter of the conscious mind and allowing the light of intuition to come to the surface. At first glance this method seems easier but in reality it is every bit as exacting as working on a *koan*. It is a skill which has been lost, and must be slowly and patiently regained:

> *Za-zen* is not . . . sitting with a blank mind which excludes all the impressions of the inner and outer senses. It is not 'concentration' in the usual sense of restricting the attention to a single sense object, such as a point of light or the tip of one's nose. It is simply a quiet awareness, without comment, of whatever happens to be here and now. This awareness is attended by the most vivid sensation of 'nondifference' between oneself and the external world, between the mind and its contents—the various sounds, sights, and other impressions of the surrounding environment.[20]

The reasoning behind 'quiet sitting' as a way to Enlightenment is quite simple: as one is *already* a Buddha, an 'Enlightened One', there is no need to try to become one through any kind of effort. The truth, of course, is that neither method is exclusively right. And it seems that, depending on the individual psychology of each student, they will both produce the liberation sought for, the moment of *satori*, the 'atom of delight'. In the end, one realises that there is no need for any 'method', for what is important in Zen is the development of a radically new way of seeing and relating to the world:

> At one stroke I forgot all my knowledge!
> There's no use for artificial discipline,
> For, move as I will, I manifest the ancient Way.[21]

Neil Gunn's intuitive awareness of this, and his vision of the other, more vital, landscape of delight is thus fully in keeping with the spirit of Zen.

The vision of the world as a realm of light and delight is no evasion of reality. As is perfectly clear from the *Saltire Review* articles of 1958–9, the concept of delight fully comprehends that initial sense of fear and panic induced by the experience of going beyond the conscious self:

> Have you ever, as a small boy, wandered farther from home than you meant to or were aware of—say, up a strath or valley—until you found yourself in a place where you had never been before? All at once you realise that *you* are in this strange place. Stock still, not breathing so that you can listen, you stare at grey rocks with whorls of lichen on them like faces, tree-roots like snakes, the trees themselves heavy with leaves and silent. Your heart comes into your throat. Quietly, very quietly, you get back onto the path, then take to your toes for all you are worth. This may have been the first experience of panic fear—the first meeting with the old Greek god. But you also met someone else there, much nearer to you than Pan: you met yourself.[22]

This 'panic fear' is an integral part of the experience, and is similar to the 'doubt sensation' which is an important precondition for the Zen experience of *satori*. The step out of the familiar ego into the unknown self can only be made with great effort, and Gunn realises the need to follow this experience through, to the freedom beyond the fear:

> Normally at this point one gets back into the old familiar places as quickly as possible. But if the surprise, the shock, of finding oneself in such new and surprising scenery is great enough, there may be induced the involuntary reflection: That I should be here! I—here—amid the strange and bewildering! At such a moment, if the shock has really been astonishing enough, the 'I' has a new feel, a new taste. It is in a way as if one had never really met this 'I' before.[23]

14

This discovery of a new 'feel' to the self is the crux of the experience. In *The Atom of Delight* Gunn called it the finding of the 'second self'. The discovery is memorable:

> For the real point of the experience is that one comes upon oneself, the 'I', as one may never have done before, almost as though it were outside onself, in a detachment evoked by the strangeness of the scene and the moment. In this sense it is objective not subjective. One apprehends one's presence there as one might the presence of a stranger. And the experience is incredibly refreshing, cool as birch-scented air, and full of wonder.[24]

This is the atom of delight, the moment of *satori*, that takes understanding beyond the workings of the conscious and limited intellect. The finding of the second self is rare and is characterised by a sense of wholeness and integration: 'Not broken bits falling apart, but a calm cohering whole. Not fear but assurance. Not terror but delight.'[25]

The delight comes as part of the awareness that one is not something separate, and therefore in a certain degree alienated from the world in which one lives. Gunn's vision of the world as a realm of delight is a vision of the world as seen in the light of a wisdom that transcends the subjectivity of the individual ego. This delight is not the opposite of some other quality such as pain or misery, but is a state beyond the dualities of conventional thought. The landscape of delight, the 'other landscape' of Gunn's last novel, is a landscape seen when the intuitive function of the mind is brought into play so as to balance the power of the rational intellect. Intellect, of course, is not abandoned, but is simply incorporated within a more comprehensive vision of man than is common in the West today as Gunn points out in *The Atom of Delight*:

> . . . reason has tended to collar intellect in our time . . . For reason knows that we all want to have reason on our side. But once we have seen reason plain, we can use it as the wonderful tool it is, and then get on with the real business of being alive along the way whose milestones are momentary or timeless experiences of being whole—mind, body and hand—in the delight that is memorable and breathe an immemorial air. (p.291)

And earlier in *The Atom of Delight*, while thinking of his childhood, Gunn had recalled how an involvement in games had led him to an early awareness of the relative value of rational thought:

> . . . the inner body had its seat of government, so had the hand, and so had thought. In action thought was the slowest of the three and at times had to be told to keep out of the way and mind its own business. Logic and delight did not always cohabit, though logic had its delights. (p.131)

He describes this process of learning to trust the intuitive mind in the article 'Light'. Part of that description has already been quoted above, but the full quotation shows how in this process the rational faculties of the mind are not simply abandoned:

> But it's the next and final step that's the difficult one—and really quite impossible to describe because of its unique nature . . . In the end thought itself gets choked and the mind becomes a void. It's at this point that the miracle happens, and the void, the void itself, gets lit up: the light spreads, burgeons; it is suffused with wonder, delight, a miraculous sense of freedom. And then you become aware of your self there, aware of a rare self, the rare self that interpenetrates all, sees and knows with a final certainty. I know some such self has been spelt with a capital S, just as the word certainly has been called Truth or Reality. But I don't want in this practical exercise to use capitals, or words like Mysticism, Transcendence and so on. There is no need; only a little application, persistence, failure and more persistence. The way is open. But one must go along it far enough for thought to get blocked and the void of no-thought to open out, for only then can enlightenment come.[26]

'The way is open.' This is the Zen image of the Gateless Gate. In other words man is already Enlightened. To realise this fully all he must do is to cease thinking of Enlightenment as something other, something for which he must strive. Enlightenment is not for an élite but is something that happens to everyone, if only they approach life in the right frame of mind. This is an idea that runs all through Gunn's work. Always it is asserted that the glimpse of the other landscape, the breakthrough to Enlightenment, is not so rare as is normally imagined. He is careful to point out that there are degrees of Enlightenment, and that the Zen experience is of greater intensity than that of someone living a 'normal' life. That, after all, is why there are Zen monasteries, organised as they are, with extensive periods of sitting meditation and the solving of *koans*. But this in no way demeans whatever degree of Enlightenment might be attained by a person living within his own community, and seeking some kind of order in his life. This fact is also fully recognised by Zen masters and commentators, despite their insistence on the abruptness and certainty of *satori*.

For Neil Gunn each flash of awareness, however seemingly insignificant in itself, is a guide to the realm of delight, a signpost on the Way which is Tao. Approached in this way the whole of life then becomes transformed into a marvellous 'poaching expedition to the source of delight':

> Intuitions of varying degrees of vision and scope come and go, but I am convinced they leave something of themselves behind, and this something gets reinforced every time an intuition is recollected with its original clarity and freshness, and because of this it casts its blessings on the new incident or situation that evoked it. Thus its own small world of delight spreads.
>
> Finally, then, an exercise in concentration, meditation and contemplation increases the chances of being struck by intuitions, intuitions on the way to a final enlightenment . . .[27]

In *The Atom of Delight* Gunn clearly demonstrated the importance he placed on this way of seeing in his life and in his art. Yet in spite of this many critics of his work regard it as an eccentric late 'influence' which diverted his energies from the depiction of what one writer calls 'essential Highland experience'.[28] Such an attitude, though, seems unnecessarily to limit our understanding of the real nature of Gunn's achievement, because for him there was no split between the ordinary world of everyday experience and the 'other landscape' of delight. The following chapters are an attempt to open up this area of 'light, delight, and Zen' for readers of Gunn's fiction. There is

17

no attempt to be exhaustive. Rather I have concentrated on discussing seven of Gunn's novels in chronological order so as to give some idea of the scope and development of this aspect of his fiction. Simultaneously each chapter is concerned with a different aspect of the process of meditation which is central to both Zen and Taoism, so that the reader is made aware of Gunn's interest in Eastern philosophy as a living reality and not merely as an intellectual concept.

THE PIVOT OF TAO
Butcher's Broom 1934

The practice of meditation develops in the individual a quality of mind and action that is imbued with the spontaneity (*tzu-jan*) of Tao itself, the natural Way of things. It is a state of being that admits of no separation between man and the world. Seen from the standpoint of wisdom, man is co-extensive with the natural world, and part of a larger process. As such he cannot regard it 'objectively'. The attempt to do so is pointless because in this, Zen says, man is like 'an eye that sees but cannot see itself', and the split thus induced between man and environment is potentially destructive as it disturbs the natural balance of Tao. Sadly, however, it is on this level that most of us live for the greater part of our lives, only attaining to our original wholeness of thought and action in brief flashes.

In the East it has long been recognised that the world is not an arbitrary collection of separate 'things', but rather that it is an organic process in which each different thing or event has its part to play, and that although the pattern may be interfered with it cannot be directed from outside without disrupting its natural order. In the West, however, this is only now being discovered, largely through the extraordinary vision of the world being revealed to us as a result of the advances made by twentieth-century physics. It may be some time before the new perspectives gained in this science begin to be felt in everyday life in the West, but the vision of the organic universe underlies the whole of Chinese philosophy. To the Chinese the world is an organic network of intersecting and interacting forces which

19

find their own natural balance. In this organic view of the world the individual is not seen as separate from his surroundings, but rather as being an invaluable part of the one continuous process. To the Chinese this process is Tao.

> The manifest world is in a perpetual state of flux, or transitoriness. It is the ever-moving, ever-changing and there is nothing fixed or permanent in the phenomenal world, all its possibilities are contained in growth and only growth can reveal life.[1]

And the business of life, according to Chinese philosophy, is not to try and conquer this flux by attempting to straighten out its inconsistencies and paradoxes, but to learn instead how best to work with the process and so achieve results by utilising the natural flow of events. This learning is the process of meditation.

The open-minded and creative attitude of meditation allows man to live within this flux with no sense of alienation, because it teaches him to understand the conflicting forces which make up his own personality and so helps him to find a stable centre common to himself and to the world beyond.

> Meditation . . . is among other things a learning to still the mind, to control it, to centre the mind's potential energy. In this quietness or condensation of the mind's energy, the mind expands and is capable of producing more acute realizations. Consequently, and in time, the body and mind seem to come together in a harmony or a centring because separateness, or duality, of the body and mind is diminished and at times even absent. It seems, in essence, that it is this separateness of body and mind which prevents humans from knowing their true self and is consequently the source of much struggle, of much unhappiness, of much suffering.[2]

This quest for balance, for life's still centre, is one of the major themes of Neil Gunn's fiction. It appears again and again in different guises, and each time something is added to our understanding because it is not a theme which is introduced merely as an interesting idea, but it is something which is central to human experience—the need to evolve a balanced approach to life so that our own lives can evolve and develop creatively instead of being a series of meaningless confrontations. For Gunn, one of the most potent symbols of such a way of life was the traditional Gaelic culture of Scotland, a culture which is described in *The Lost Chart* as 'a remarkable civilization . . . perhaps particularly remarkable in this that it informed even its superstitions, its charms for healing cattle, with that ultimate power which pervades the universe and which they knew, at once profoundly and simply, as the power of God.' (p.180)

This way of life had largely passed by the time of Gunn's birth; in part destroyed by the Clearances, in part dying out naturally as all civilisations do in time. But enough of it remained unconsciously in the behaviour of the people among whom he grew up for Gunn to recognise something of its original nature, and to employ this to telling effect in his fiction. Nowhere is this more obvious than in *Butcher's Broom* (1934).

In *Butcher's Broom* the traditional Gaelic way of life as it is embodied in the timeless figure of Mairi counterpoints the violent social change which is taking place elsewhere. In the end, of course, the ritualised pattern of the traditional way of life is destroyed with the onset of the Clearances, and is replaced by the 'modern' world of improvements and progress. And yet, as Gunn shows, even after Mairi's death something vital remains; a creative attitude of mind which is not taken in by the illusion of progress and which survives because of an inner resilience which is the process of life itself, always ready to grow and develop, never thinking it knows all the answers. By the end of the novel this attitude has been passed on from Mairi to the young woman Elie, who is left to carry on living in the violent and chaotic world of the Clearances, with her son and her wounded husband to look after.

Although the tragedy of the Clearances and their effects on the Highlands lie behind the surface reality of many of Gunn's novels, *Butcher's Broom* is the only one of the novels to treat the Clearances explicitly. But the novel does not merely set out to fictionalise events and personages of the historical Sutherland Clearances. As in the other two major Clearance novels, Fionn MacColla's *And the Cock Crew*, and Iain Crichton Smith's *Consider the Lilies*, it is clear that however much the Clearances are there as historical fact, they also function as a symbol of one of man's central psychological problems—the relationship between the creative and the destructive elements of his psyche.

> There would seem to be a power in nature that once set on harrying is not content to defeat and break, but must with malignant intensity pursue its quarry into a physical death of revolting and bloody cruelty. (p.21)

> Now when any man opposes the fundamental principle of life in another, he must, by the irksome consciousness or sub-consciousness of what he is doing, become antagonistic and violent, and will hunt about in the other's life for what he can despise and hate. (p.268)

This last comes after a passage which clearly indicates Gunn's awareness of his use of the Clearances as symbolic of man's destructive potential. What is enacted in the Clearances is a clash of totally divergent ways of life and ideas of human value:

> For the cleavage between the desires of the people and the desires of the landlord was fundamental and could never be bridged. On the people's part there was love of the land, love of its visible features as something near and natural to them as their own limbs; they grew out of it as a birch tree grows out of it, and could be removed only by a tearing up of roots . . .
> Opposed to this on the part of the landlord and his factors was the conception of material gain arranged in a pattern called Progress. That this progress has proved illusory merely destroys the name they gave to their excuse, and strips their lust for possession to its naked strength. (pp.267–8)

Throughout Gunn's fiction Gaelic culture is used as a symbol of life and creativity. Although he was fully aware that the distinctive values he saw operative within Gaelic culture were in decline at the time of which he was writing he still believed that the Gaelic way of life was superior to that of the evictors in the sense that its main concern was with the good of the community as a whole and not with the self-centred pursuit of individual wealth which was a prime motivation of the evictors. Gunn's picture of this society shows, even in decline, a

22

remarkable range and diversity—from Mairi's vital knowledge of medicine and of things of the body, to the subtle skills of singer and musician in dealing with matters of the spirit. One value, however, stands out—the respect accorded to each man's individuality.

In part this arose out of the closeness of the people's contact with nature. Individual lives were seen as part of a larger, more comprehensive process. In *The Atom of Delight*, talking of his own boyhood in Caithness, Gunn says that this attitude could still be found in Highland communities at the beginning of this century. And this he explains with reference to the old clan system:

> The social structure was so simple that it didn't consciously exist . . .
>
> Perhaps this 'classless' feeling came out of the old Gaelic clan system, wherein the chief was not a landlord but a leader, the head of the tribe, the father of the clan or *clann*, the children. In the Latin tag, he was *primus inter pares*, the first among equals . . .
>
> In his own place, the boy had no chief, though it was in the region of the old clan territory . . .
>
> And the people got on very well without a chief. The old feeling of equality among themselves remained, of that independence which being dependence on oneself was not directed against any other but, on the contrary, respected a similar independence in all others. (pp.117–19)

The clan-based society was for Gunn an image of a society in which each man was free by virtue of having his own place in that society, with his own valued contribution to make. The modern phenomenon of alienation had no hold in such a society.

In *Butcher's Broom* he attempted to give some sense of the value of a way of life which, at the time of writing, had been largely lost and which even at the time in which he set the novel had been in decline. The story centres on the house of Mairi, the healer of a Sutherland community, and explores the interrelationships of the various people connected with her. Her grandson Davie, and Elie, a young woman of the village, live with her. Throughout the novel the various developing relationships between these three characters help to lift the novel beyond a mere portrayal of the larger historical drama of which their lives are part. Only the character of Mairi remains static—for reasons that will emerge later. Elie falls in love with a young man Colin, who leaves to go to war unaware that she is pregnant by him. Elie leaves to have her child in the Lowlands in secrecy. For eight years she wanders, destitute, before returning with her son Colin to the Riasgan and to Mairi. On her return Davie, no longer a boy, is able to see Elie as the attractive young woman she is, and Gunn makes much of the ambivalence of their attitudes to each other. This is further complicated when Elie marries Rob the miller late in the novel and also by Davie's attraction to a girl of his own age. These various male/female relationships echo and develop many of the concerns of the central relationship between Elie and Colin.

The community to which Elie returns is living under the imminent threat of eviction in order to make room on the land for sheep. And perhaps the central relationship of the book after her return is that between her and Mairi—a relationship which enables her to endure the harshness of the evictions and to assert the positive values of life in a situation which appears to others hopeless. The people of the Riasgan are cleared to the shore where life is all but impossible for them. The novel ends when Mairi is killed by a shepherd's dog, an image which encapsulates the death of a culture. But the novel is not pessimistic. Elie's son Colin, and his father, who has returned wounded from the war, meet for the first time and take care of the body. They do not recognise each other, but carry out the task as a communal sharing of the burden, so continuing in some degree to uphold the traditional values which Mairi has represented throughout the book.

As the novel opens we see Mairi at her work of gathering herbs for her healing art, and throughout this first chapter, which follows Mairi about her business, and back to her home in the Riasgan, the reader's perspective on the action is continually changed and modified under the directions of the narrator. From seeing Mairi as a small human figure among hills and sea and sky, we move close enough to perceive the

24

'vacant glitter' of her eyes, and then right inside her mind. The movement is not simply one of 'homing-in', however, and almost as soon as we enter Mairi's stream-of-consciousness we leave it to catch another glimpse of her solitary human figure making its homeward journey through a wild landscape. Even the apparent solidity of the land itself is seen to be continually in motion—a movement in both time and space:

> These outlines and these hills, the winding valley, the many valleys, the breasts of the hills, the little birch woods, the knolls, the humps and hillocks and boulders, the gravel faces, the black bogs, and always for movement the streams winding like snakes in the green or grey-green bottoms. To know one valley amongst these northern uplands was to know all. That was true! As Mairi might say with her thin polite smile. And she might even act as though she believed it. For there are times when all persons are beings moving about in a valley and looking from a little distance as different from one another as does not matter. And no irony is caught in the eye that stares unwinkingly and, throwing the valley itself out of focus in space, makes it change and curve in the backflow of time.
>
> The backflow of time that is frozen at last in the Ice Age. The ice moves forward and time slowly returns. Vast hollows are gouged out and mountains are planed smooth; seas appear. But the work is rough and the glacier comes again and again. Until the valley is shaped as the eyes of Dark Mairi see it. A smooth shape of slender flanks and fluent spinal ridges, of swelling breasts and wandering arms, brown-skinned except where the region of its fertility lies softly grey-green with grass. Here men and women are at work, concerned forever, too, with fertility in that place and in themselves; turning the earth over and sowing grain seed in it, harvesting, and rearing flocks and herds; making love in youth and story-telling in old age, with a music distilled out of it all as singular and memoried as dark-brown honey. A life shaggy as the legs of an animal, shaggy and tough, with clear eyes above and wary nostrils; and night a small den where the whole body curls in its own thick warmth.
>
> But it is like that perhaps only in thought at a distance; near at hand it is quite suddenly the face of a young woman with its virgin clearness, that brimming clearness forever waiting to be troubled . . . (pp.11–12)

This continual movement which not only distorts visual perspective, but which fuses the abstract and concrete qualities of the scene conveys a strong impression of the landscape as something alive. To borrow MacDiarmid's phrase, 'the haill thing kelters like a theatre claith'. The vision of the world as alive and continually changing finds analogues in Eastern philosophies, and in twentieth-century physics.

> The more one studies the religious and philosophical texts of the Hindus, Buddhists and Taoists, the more it becomes apparent that in all of them the world is conceived in terms of movement, flow and change. This dynamic quality of Eastern philosophy seems to be one of its most important features. The Eastern mystic sees the universe as an inseparable web, whose interconnections are dynamic and not static. The cosmic web is alive; it moves, grows and changes continually. Modern physics, too, has come to conceive of the universe as such a web of relations and, like Eastern mysticism, has recognized that this web is intrinsically dynamic. The dynamic aspect of matter arises in quantum theory as a consequence of the wave-nature of subatomic particles, and is even more essential in relativity theory . . . where the unification of space and time implies that the being of matter cannot be separated from its activity. The properties of subatomic particles can therefore only be understood in a dynamic context; in terms of movement interaction and transformation.[3]

To see the world in this way leads to a radical redefinition of self. In *Butcher's Broom* the fluidity of the natural landscape extends to the breaking down of the normal boundaries of identity. On one occasion the character of Elie merges with that of Seumas og, a man with the second sight:

> Seumas og had neither spoken nor looked at Elie since she had entered, but had remained seated and bent towards the fire. Elie began to feel the drooping curve of her body, and all at once it was she who was there by the fire, and a sensation of such grey hopelessness beset her that she broke her body back and glanced about her, struggling to escape. (p.97)

And in *Butcher's Broom* Gunn attempts to show how the Gael was aware of this different sense of self, on a purely practical and not on a 'mystical' level. The political organisation of the clan allowed each person a fully-integrated place within his society. If every individual is a manifestation of the one eternal and infinite being, then so each clan member is a manifestation of the clan. The same life-force connects him to his chief—an analogy brought closer by the etymology of *clann*, the Gaelic for 'children'.

Central to this aspect of the novel is the relationship between Mairi and Elie, and behind this the conception of the land itself as female. We have already seen the land described as a woman's body, and throughout *Butcher's Broom* there is a coherent pattern of imagery which links the ideas of land/woman/fertility/receptivity and creativity. The Gaelic culture also is part of this pattern of imagery, shown as growing out of this land 'as a birch tree grows out of it', while the evictors' attitude to the land is purely destructive because they have no real contact with it. Further, within the Gaelic society itself, it is the women who stand out as holding some hope for the future.

If we look closer at Mairi and Elie we come right to the heart of the book. These two characters symbolise two very different aspects of the earth—its continually evolving flux, and the still point around which that flux revolves. Elie is consistently described in images of softness, of flowing movement, and of brownness linking her with the brown-skinned limbs of the earth-woman of Chapter 1:

> Elie's breasts were soft and full; her shoulders tilted upward or drooped, her body had a flowing movement that would come at one with an intimate wheedling voice wanting the fun of breaking away into pieces of teased laughter. But Mairi was tight and upright as a standing stone; she was like an earth outcrop to Elie's brown stream. (pp. 25–6)

All the images describing Mairi on the other hand are images of persistence, of rootedness. And it is clear that Mairi, repository of the traditions of the Gaelic way of life, symbolises that centre or core of life which Eliot called 'the still point of the turning world'. Mairi is 'still', not because she ignores the flux of the world, but rather because she has fully come to terms with this flux. Her rootedness is not antagonistic to the flow of change,

27

but, paradoxically, is part of that flow, a concept that may be explained with reference to the *I Ching* or *Book of Changes*, the ancient Chinese Classic, with its acceptance of 'nonchange' as a form of change.

> In the *Book of Changes* a distinction is made between three kinds of change: nonchange, cyclic change, and sequent change. Nonchange is the background, as it were, against which change is made possible. For in regard to any change there must be some fixed point to which the change can be referred; otherwise there can be no definite order and everything is dissolved in chaotic movement . . . The ultimate frame of reference for all that changes is the nonchanging.[4]

As the relationship between Elie and Mairi evolves we can see how Elie grows to recognise the importance of such a still centre in the life of each individual and not just in the larger unit of society. The movement of *Butcher's Broom* shows how through contact with Mairi she attains her own still centre, enriching her own personality, thus symbolising the persistence of the Gaelic spirit even after the Clearances.

Mairi as healer is central. With her intimate knowledge of the earth and its beneficence, she is seen as a prominent member of her society. But she is also the Earth Mother herself—the force that lives and moves through the land ensuring fertility and life. She is a fascinating mixture of symbol and actuality and an enigma even to her own people who like her well enough yet are not quite sure of her:

> Dark Mairi was like a bit of the earth that was given hands and eyes; that took from the earth and the edges of the sea healing weeds and herbs; Dark Mairi of the Shore.
>
> No one thought of her as a witch, yet there was an odd half-hinted, half-jocular conception of her as a being that went in and out of the earth, as a dark sea-beast can go out and in the caves of the ocean. Her shadow was sometimes seen when she wasn't there herself; and often her still face frightened boys in the wood. (p.150)

But time and again the narrator stresses the *practical* nature of Mairi's accomplishments. And it gradually becomes clear that

Mairi is seen in this half-frightened way by a people who have forgotten the knowledge she alone now possesses. This is especially clear when, after the people have been cleared from the Riasgan to the shore, they begin to shun Mairi, seeing her as a 'magician'. They are afraid of her, and seek her help only when desperate.

Mairi herself embodies the integrated nature of the Gaelic culture in its purity. Her knowledge reconciles the ordinary and the extraordinary, allowing her to see the world more clearly. Mairi is not, like others, held back by fear of the unknown, of the irrational, because she understands how much of the irrational there is in her own being. This she has learned from a thorough awareness of the traditions of her people, and through her own particular mastery of healing which has given her a deep and lasting awareness of the processes of life. Late in the novel she goes to gather plants from which to make dyes, and we are afforded a glimpse of the world as Mairi herself sees it. Once again we are made aware of the movement of the natural world and we can see, moreover, that for Mairi the world is not a static collection of objects but is an integrated web of relationships. Each thing is distinct, yet each exists only in relation to some other.

> But Mairi knew the earth at once in a more magical and practical way than that. She saw bright crimson in white lichen and bright red in the rue root; violet in the bitter vetch, dark orange in the bramble, and purple in the sundew; yellow lay hid in the bracken root and bright yellow in the bog myrtle; scarlet dripped from the tormentil and clots of black from the dock root; 'human flesh' lay sheathed in the suave willow bark. But the lichens that spread over stone and rock provided her with her greatest treasures in scarlets and browns and in reds more vivid than blood. (pp.318–19)

This is the world as Mairi sees it—'this bright world which the human eye obscures to grey or brown of the pallor of roots'. It is a description of the landscape which lies behind our habitual dullness of perception—the other landscape of delight, vivid and unforgettable.

Gunn once told Professor Hart that he knew exactly where the character of Mairi came from:

> I was at a *ceilidh* of a sort in Inverness one night. Women were doing waulking songs and so on, and I watched them, but there was a woman there who simply sat forward in her chair—she was in her sixties, but she had straight black hair that was pulled straight back from her forehead, and her cheekbones slanted straight down back below her ears, and a little smile on her face, and this woman's image simply stayed with me—and became Dark Mairi.[5]

But in Gunn's own work there are at least two important precursors of Mairi. The first is found in a brief two-line quotation in a story in *Hidden Doors* where the following couplet is ascribed to 'the old woman of Tiree':

> It is the grey rock I am,
> And the grey rain on the rock. (p.67)

The linking of 'the old woman' with the natural landscape, and the traditionally gnomic utterance seems to give an early, if unformulated, glimpse of Mairi. The other example is more substantial—the character of the Master in Gunn's previous novel, *Sun Circle*.

In that novel, set in ninth-century Caithness, the Master is the spiritual head of a primitive people. He is seen only occasionally, and for the most part the reader sees him through the eyes of various characters who regard him with awe. He is more distant from his people than Mairi is from hers, but he and the Grove where he lives and trains his disciples is the still centre of their world. He is a man of great wisdom and knowledge and, so the people believe, the possessor of occult powers.

After the people have been broken by invasion, and the Grove has been destroyed, the Master's own being becomes a refuge and a guide for them—a function carried out by Mairi in *Butcher's Broom*. After the chiefs have died in battle, the Master and Aniel his disciple are left to preserve the wholeness of the people.

The inner qualities which enable him to perform the role of healer and guardian are evoked in *Sun Circle* in much the same way that Gunn evokes those same qualities in Mairi:

> Before (Aniel) entered the Grove, he came on the Master sitting on a turf bank. The small body was like a part of the bank, an outcrop of the ancient earth. The face was so old that its beginning was lost in the ages. The skin was the colour and texture of a scraped sheepskin that, drying in the sun, had been forgotten. And blindness veiled the eyes of the sun. When the eyes were steady for a long time they looked quite blind, but when they shifted and focussed, the breast had the melting sensation of transparence before them. Nor did turning away help, for their look was apprehended in the spine. (p.113)

The merging with the earth and the metaphoric blindness are also associated with Mairi throughout *Butcher's Broom*, but the relation between these and Mairi's 'deep sources of energy' is not rendered quite so explicitly as it is in the case of the Master. The Master is a spiritual teacher and his role as such has been summed up succinctly by Marie-Hélène Rescanières: 'The Master is a symbol of clarity, ultimately an example to others, helping them to draw their own circles of light about themselves.'[6]

Gunn's own recognition of this function is made apparent later in *Sun Circle*:

> As the Sun put a circle round the earth and all that it contained, so a man by his vision put a circle round himself. At the centre of this circle his spirit sat, and the centre of his spirit was a serenity ever watchful. Sometimes the watchfulness gave an edged joy in holding at bay the demons and even the vengeful lesser gods, and sometimes it merged with the Sun's light into pure timeless joy. (pp.365–6)

This circle with stillness at its core is a universal symbol of meditation. It is, in effect, a *mandala* and as such is an image of man's archetypal quest for wholeness and integration. C. G. Jung, in his commentary on *The Secret of the Golden Flower*, has explained how contemplation of a *mandala* can remove barriers and bring Enlightenment:

. . . the *mandala* symbol is not only a means of expression, but works an effect. It reacts upon its maker. Very ancient magical effects are associated with this symbol because it comes originally from the 'enclosing circle', the 'charmed circle', the magic of which has been preserved in countless folk-customs. The picture has the obvious purpose of drawing a *sulcus primigenius*, a magical furrow around the centre, the *templum*, or *temenos* (sacred precincts), of the innermost personality, in order to prevent 'emanation', or to guard by apotropoaeic [sic] means, deflections through external influences. Magical practices are nothing but the projection of psychic events, which, in cases like these, exert a counter influence on the soul, and act like a kind of enchantment of one's own personality. That is to say, by means of these concrete performances, the attention, or better said, the interest, is brought back to an inner, sacred domain, which is the source and goal of the soul. This inner domain contains the unity of life and consciousness, which, though once possessed, has been lost, and must now be found again.[7]

Butcher's Broom, with Mairi as the still centre in a world of continual movement and change, clearly reveals this pattern, and in this way the use of Mairi and of the traditional Gaelic culture as a symbol of man's inherent creative potential goes beyond the attempt to reproduce accurately historical events. *Butcher's Broom* is concerned with the dichotomy between two approaches to life: the creative, represented by Mairi and Elie; and the destructive, represented by the evictors. This dichotomy is representative of the struggle within each individual between his creative and his destructive impulses, and each individual's quest for the still centre in which these can find a balance.

This is the eternal opposition of *yin* and *yang*, an opposition that on closer scrutiny reveals an implicit unity. This deeper unity is perceived by the exercise of direct intuition, which places man on what Chuang Tsu calls 'the pivot of Tao':

Tao is obscured when men understand only one of a pair of opposites, or concentrate only on a partial aspect of being . . .

The pivot of Tao passes through the center where all affirmations and denials converge. He who grasps the pivot is at the stillpoint from which all movements and oppositions can be seen in their right relationship.[8]

It is clear in *Butcher's Broom* that behind the apparent chaos of life Gunn perceives an ultimate unity, and that characters, events, and objects are all aspects of this central unity. The continually changing landscape is a manifestation of cosmic energy, and if we recall Mairi's vision of the natural world in terms of the vivid colours of plants there is a strong impression of one life pulsing through all the various plants she sees—an impression conveyed by references to the flow of the blood-stream, again linking the land with the human body.

This clearer perception, the ability to see the 'changes' of the universe, and thus to be able to control these forces, leads to a more harmonious existence:

> Since in this way man comes to resemble heaven and earth, he is not in conflict with them. His wisdom embraces all things, and his Tao brings order into the whole world; therefore he does not err. He is active everywhere but does not let himself be carried away. He rejoices in heaven and has knowledge of fate, therefore he is free of care. He is content with his circumstances and genuine in his kindness, therefore he can practice love.[9]

The description could be applied equally to Mairi and to the Master. It describes precisely the basis of their powerful quietude. Both are spiritual teachers. As the Master teaches Aniel in *Sun Circle*, so Mairi teaches Elie in *Butcher's Broom*. The main difference of course is that in *Butcher's Broom* the teaching process is removed from the arcane and esoteric world of the Grove, and is embodied in a much more human contact—so much so that Elie learns almost unconsciously from Mairi. What she learns is not a doctrine or a theoretical approach to life but rather the capacity to remain 'centred' and calm in the face of all eventualities. This Mairi teaches her by the example of her own being, and Elie also contributes to this learning process through her attempts to understand Mairi.

Elie's relationship with Mairi is ambivalent, a detail caught nicely by Gunn. She is naturally drawn to Mairi but at the same time is repelled by something in Mairi's attitude which she sees as unfeeling, a callousness and a cynicism towards the joy of life.

> Elie glanced at the short but firm body, with the black head small
> and set to the neck with poise. It showed less outward emotion
> than an animal. Self-contained, it was without the expressiveness
> of sentiment and almost completely without humour. To some-
> thing in that deep negativeness, Elie's heart also responded, as it
> might in other circumstances to a bank or a tree, or to the black
> heart of the earth. (p.81)

This ambivalent attitude is at its strongest in the earlier part of
the novel where Elie and Colin are becoming increasingly aware
of their feelings for each other.

When the boys, including Colin, have decided to set off for
the war Mairi's matter-of-fact interest in this irritates Elie who
experiences a sudden and violent revulsion against her: 'A
witless woman with no more feeling than a stone. Elie hated
her; wanted to flee from her; had an awful divination of her
right to the empty core.' (pp.100–1). But in her abject misery at
the thought of losing Colin, Elie finds her solace in the earth,
through direct intuition of its affinities with Mairi, and this
particularly through an awareness of what she had just called
'the empty core'.

> In a hole like an animal's den she drew up her knees. 'I'm tired,'
> she whined. And there she lay with herself, whimpering and
> licking her sores . . .
>   But at last a stupor of exhaustion did creep over her, and the
> earth, damp and cold, pressed against hip and shoulder . . .
>   Something of this misery and stupor of the earth was with her
> when, in the first of the dusk, she crept shivering from that den
> and went down towards the hollow by the wood. Yet the earth in
> its stupor had a strange, liberating quality; a mindlessness, an
> end. Black peaty ooze, small hoof-marks, crushed ·dung, thin
> heath tough as wire, broken contorted rock, grey lichen every-
> where like the frost of death. (p.101)

Again the writing is at once naturalistic and symbolic. Elie is
pictured as a wounded animal in its den. Exhaustion comes
upon her naturally enough after the intense internal conflict of
the previous few days, and she feels the solidity of the earth as
comforting. But it is not an easy comfort. The earth is damp,
and cold enough to make her shiver. It allows no room for self-

pity. Contact with its impassive neutrality forces Elie to assess her position realistically, just as Mairi's peculiar vacancy does. Elie's stupor, the stupor of the earth, and Mairi's detachment are all inextricably linked.

That such moments had particular associations in Neil Gunn's mind is clear from the fact that the setting and substance of the incident is apparent in the story 'Such Stuff as Dreams', published in *Hidden Doors*, his first collection of stories in 1929, and also in *Highland River* where the black peaty ooze, small hoof-marks, and crushed dung of the earth are seen with similar intensity by Kenn in his meditation on the moor at the end of his quest. The moment is a breakthrough to the stillness at the core of life, the constancy at the heart of change. This movement from a state of utter misery to a calm acceptance of life as delight, the one emerging naturally out of the other is an illustration of the belief that 'reversal is the movement of Tao', that once something reaches an extreme it changes into its opposite, the cyclic flow of *yin* and *yang*. In going beyond self-pity Elie has learned to see her situation differently, has learned to respond spontaneously, without the need for egocentric reflection.

Reaching through to the emptiness of the earth has led her to an understanding of the emptiness of her own idea of her 'self'. *The Heart Sutra*, a central Zen text says, 'Form is Emptiness and Emptiness is Form'. And this is the state of mind which Zen Buddhists call 'no-mind' (*wu-hsin*). Its significance has been described by the modern Zen master Sokei-an Sasaki:

One day I wiped out all the notions from my mind. I gave up all desire. I discarded all the words with which I thought and stayed in quietude. I felt a little queer—as if I were being carried into something, or as if I were touching some power unknown to me . . . and Ztt! I entered. I lost the boundary of my physical body. I had my skin, of course, but I felt I was standing in the centre of the cosmos. I spoke, but my words had lost their meaning. I saw people coming towards me, but all were the same man. All were myself! I had never known this world. I had believed that I was created, but now I must change my opinion: I was never created; I was the cosmos; no individual Mr Sasaki existed.[10]

This reorientation allows one to channel one's energies creatively, in marked contrast to the rather fragmented way in which we normally act. In Elie's case it issues in an intensification of her love for Colin.

> When in the hollow Elie met Colin, she rose from the bed of the moor to his warmth. There was nothing querulous left in her. Her love, turned from the doubts of life, rose up complete and unquestioning. At first her ardour frightened him a little, and the crush of her arms choked and hurt his throat, but he felt her escaping from something, full of an insatiable hunger that must bite into him. He remonstrated, half laughing. But her ardour acted on his own strength which rose to meet hers. She held against him till her strength broke. It was the first serpent bite in the innocence of their love.
>
> In this denial of past and future, Elie found freedom, and in its perfect desperation became more variable and attractive than she had ever been. (p.102)

Giving up the illusion of a separate and solid 'self' Elie enters fully the fluid world of delight, and there finds her true self—that part of her that has always been in contact with the unconscious processes of life. The passage is remarkable in the way it relates this new sense of self to the awakening in Elie of sexual awareness.

Elie's openness is a strange new feeling, one which Colin does not quite understand. Elie herself has shaken off the *need* to understand; 'Her love . . . rose up complete and unquestioning'. Colin's anxiety is a distortion of the awe and wonder which this new awareness engenders—an idea also powerfully expressed by MacDiarmid in *A Drunk Man Looks at the Thistle*:

> A luvin' wumman is a licht
> That shows a man his waefu' plicht,
> Bleezin' steady on ilka bane,
> Wrigglin' sinnen an' twinin' vein,
> Or fleerin' quick an' gane again,
> And the mair scunnersome the sicht
> The mair for love and licht he's fain
> Till clear and chitterin' and nesh
> Move a' the miseries o' his flesh . . .

36

O lass, wha see'est me
As I daur hardly see,
I marvel that your bonny een
Are as they hadna seen.[11]

The link between sexual awareness and renewed self-awareness is widely recognised, and it is an important theme in many of Gunn's novels. In *Butcher's Broom* it is closely allied to the idea of the complementary role of opposites, as outlined in a description of the economy of the Riasgan in terms of labour, and the way this changed with the changing seasons:

> The women were the more persistent and fruitful workers, and found the males frequently in their way. Many of the tasks about a house they would not let a man perform—even if he had wanted to, which, of course, he did not. In this matter of work there was so strong a custom that if a man did a woman's work, where a woman was fit to do it, the feeling of shamed surprise would be felt stronger by the woman than by the man. The system worked very well, for the man in his sphere and the woman in hers were each equally governing and indispensable. Thus the difference between a man and a woman was emphasised and each carried clear before the other the characteristics and mystery of the male and female sex. (p.65)

No doubt this is an idealisation, and the system like any other could be abused, but on the whole the philosophical import is clear—that life is carried on through the continual interaction of two opposite, but complementary forces; *yin* and *yang*.

The actuality of this concept is brought home to the reader in those parts of the novel which deal with the relationship between Elie and Colin:

> Occasionally Colin was frightened, and in odd lonely moments would shudder, and grasp [sic] and blot the thing out. But there was no fear in Elie at all. The days were golden. The rain was soft. She would open her lips to the rain. And however cold the wind, her body nestled from her clothes into it. (p.119)

Colin is afraid because he realises that his going away to be a soldier is a denial of something he only half understands in Elie's open sensuality. He is held in awe by something in Elie which is beyond his influence, and which has begun to influence him. The awesome qualities Elie manifests are archetypally female—receptivity, and a terrible acceptance— qualities which have long troubled man's subconscious. She faces life openly, nakedly, devoid of the male illusions of permanence, and of mankind's privileged position as 'ruler' of the world. Colin cannot face life in this way; he needs the illusion to give his life a sense of purpose and direction. Elie has gone beyond the need for such illusions and has the courage to live without them. She also has the compassion to accept that for Colin this is not possible:

> . . . a certain shyness, almost wistfulness, in his voice when he had spoken, touched her heart as no reason of his ever could. He would *like* to go. The deep craving in a boy's breast to do what other boys are doing. And beyond all the boys were the dark forces of the world, of chiefs and kings and armies, deploying on foreign or nightmare fields. (p.95)

Throughout *Butcher's Broom* Elie's attitude is contrasted with the more purposive, power-dominated male attitudes of Colin which, however rational they may appear, are based on unconscious motivation.

In this the relationship between Elie and Colin parallels the larger conflict of creative and destructive attitudes examined in the clash between the people and the evictors. It is clear that for Gunn the creative values are essentially female, in the sense that they are more intuitive than rational. Mairi and Elie in turn embody the lasting qualities of receptivity and acceptance. The attitude of the evictors, the attitude of male characters like Colin is fundamentally different, believing in the use of force to turn events to one's own advantage. And the message of *Butcher's Broom* is that only through the adoption of such 'female' attitudes will man survive. Only by giving up his almost total reliance on conscious thought, the deliberate attempt of the ego to relate everything to itself, and by developing a more open and intuitive mode of thought will man become once again harmonised with the larger rhythm of life. Then his actions will no longer go against the grain, but will follow the natural curvature of events, and his life will gain poise and balance from having found 'the pivot of Tao'.

RETURNING TO THE SOURCE
Highland River 1937

If *Sun Circle* and *Butcher's Broom*, with their emphasis on the need to find a still centre within the apparently chaotic flux of the world, provide us with an image of meditation, then *Highland River* (1937) takes us right into the heart of the meditative process itself. In *Highland River* the reader is involved immediately in what Gunn calls 'a poaching expedition to the source of delight', and the book is so structured as to ensure the reader's sympathy for the quest it describes. The movement of the book itself creates in the reader an appropriate 'apparatus of response'.

Highland River is the story of a nuclear physicist, Kenn Sutherland, who sets out to trace the source of the river of his childhood. He had grown up beside the river, played beside it, and wrestled from it a great silver salmon in the central episode of the book. The river is part of the life of the community, and in many ways is central to Kenn'šexperience as child and adolescent. Due to the close relationship between man and environment in this community, Kenn's setting out to discover the source of the river is also a quest to discover the source of his own identity, and that of the community which shaped him.

There is nothing vague or 'mystical' about his quest. It is a purely practical search for that which gives meaning and significance to life:

> What he wants to catch inside himself is something very elusive, because it is so imponderable, so without meaning or aim. Yet it

39

achieves a startling reality when caught and held—as it must be and always is—suddenly.

It is a moment of sheer unconditional delight that may not be described or explained, and that nothing can ever explain away. Delight is here not so much too strong as too uniform a word. For the moment may be troubling in the old panic sense; it may be ecstatic; or it may, by a lure of memory, evasive as a forgotten scent, draw one towards it as towards a source. (p.48)

Gunn echoed this in a letter to Hugh MacDiarmid in December 1937, where he states that while such an area may be difficult territory for the writer it is still a valid area of human experience and of art:

There are thoughts which are devilish elusive. And that elusiveness of the mind is a reality, and any writer with a mind has to do something with it or about it on paper . . . But this elusiveness is the very antithesis of vagueness. It is indeed a deliberate and difficult effort to get hold in that region where thought tends to get lost in the rarefied.[1]

Kenn himself is fully aware of the difficulty of his quest, fully aware that he is obeying an impulse which, although conscious, is hard to define and seems to be a matter of 'instinct' like the salmon's return to the waters of its birth:

. . . in recent years, the simple fact that he had never actually gone to the source of his childhood's river had quietly taken possession of his mind, and by a slowly growing impulsive need had started it on this long, intricate quest, a quest of lost times and places, but not for the mere sake of evoking them, or of indulging pleasant or sentimental memories, but of capturing or isolating a quality of awareness and delight in order to provide the core of life with warmth and light. (p.320)

This of course is the quest which Gunn described in his autobiographical work *The Atom of Delight*, published some twenty years later, the quest for 'the particular moment, the arrested scene, that holds a significance difficult to define; but not at all vague; vivid, fine with a delight that words blur; as the word significance blurs the clear *this is it*'. (p.8) The 'significance difficult to define' is the awareness that comes upon one during these moments that one is not separate from the natural world, but rather that one is an active *part* of its creative process. This realisation brings about the joy or delight of the experience, because however much doubt may set in afterwards, *at the time* we know that this renewed feeling of wholeness and integration is man's natural state:

> The central core of the experience seems to be the conviction, or insight, that the immediate *now*, whatever its nature, is the goal and fulfillment [sic] of all living. Surrounding and flowing from this insight is an emotional ecstasy, a sense of relief, freedom, and lightness . . .[2]

The ecstasy, however, is secondary to the initial insight, for 'the immediate *now* is complete even when it is not ecstatic'.[3] This sense of the experience of 'nowness' is evident in *Highland River*:

> At such a moment, eternity was felt not as a dimension in time forward in the way the mind usually feels it, nor even as a dimension in time backward, but as the point of meeting where the circle starts and ends. Time held in suspension or poise and losing all dimension in an eternal now. (p.330)

The idea that this elusive moment of insight, once experienced, draws one onward, as towards a source is a description both of the quest and the process of meditation—a process succinctly described by Lao Tsu in chapter 16 of the *Tao Te Ching*:

> Empty yourself of everything.
> Let the mind rest at peace.
> The ten thousand things rise and fall while the Self watches their return.
> They grow and flourish and then return to the source.
> Returning to the source is stillness, which is the way of nature.[4]

The story of Kenn's return to the source is the story of his gradual discovery of the way of meditation.

Gunn draws the reader into the actuality of this process by the way in which he engages his sympathy with his central character. The action of *Highland River* is related in flashback, with special emphasis on moments of particular significance—

41

'atoms of delight'. The mature Kenn reflects on the significance of these moments as he relives them in his memory, re-living them so vividly that they seem in fact not remembered but still happening. Two of the book's major themes are conveyed to the reader through this simple structural device; the illusory nature of our normal concept of time; and the illusory nature of our normal conception of self.

But in *Highland River* it is the *actuality* rather than the concepts of meditation which Gunn evokes so surely. This is achieved mainly by the way in which he catches the tone of voice of the central character, through whose consciousness the reader is made aware of the action of the book; a voice which recalls vividly many incidents, many people, from the past and is able to regard them with detachment. Kenn's thought never 'sticks' on any one incident. Always it moves on, leaving each thing in its own place, not forcing any of the issues involved. Many times Kenn's thoughts come back to himself at different stages of his life, in both admirable and not so admirable guises, which he recognises as aspects of a central core, which in communion with the natural world of the moor—the setting for his quest— experiences all. In the end Kenn's thought is stilled, and he comes upon the stillness that underlies all action. Thought can only go so far, and so this final attainment is expressed by silence: not the silence of despair, but the silence which *knows* that this stillness beyond thought is the end of all the exploring which had gone before. Through the 'action' of the novel, through contact with the gently expanding and contracting rhythms of Kenn's constantly changing vision, Gunn takes the reader very near the heart of that silence.

This process of quietly watching the mind without inter- ference, simply allowing thought to take its course until it gradually attains to stillness, is meditation. On the moor, quietly going over the events of his life, Kenn is at the heart of the *mandala* of *Highland River*. And it is this gently controlled awareness at the centre that is the difference between the meditative mind and the normal chaotic jumble which makes up our consciousness. Learning how to be aware in this way is not easy. As Kenn realises he has been on this quest since the very moment of his birth. Yet the quest is still problematic. A *Zenrin* poem highlights the difficulty:

You cannot get it by taking thought;
You cannot seek it by not taking thought.[5]

And Zen master Nan-ch'uan is more explicit:

The Tao is not a matter of knowing, nor a matter of not knowing.
To know is a delusory way of thinking, and not to know is a matter of insensibility.[6]

What is required is a state of mind that is quietly aware of the direction in which one's thoughts are tending, but does not attempt to force those thoughts along a 'better' channel. Such an attempt to direct one's thoughts is an assertion of the ego, and as such emphasises the split between man and the world—a split which the direct intuition of meditation shows to be an illusion. This insight releases the freedom of Enlightenment:

In this moment there is nothing which comes to be. In this moment there is nothing which ceases to be. Thus there is no birth-and-death to be brought to an end. Wherefore the absolute tranquillity is this present moment. Though it is at this moment, there is no limit to this moment, and herein is eternal delight.[7]

This is the creative void of Buddhism—the emptiness in which form has its being, the stillness out of which action arises. It is experienced as the state of 'no-mind' (*wu-hsin*), when all conscious thought, all the 'action' of the separate ego is ended and man becomes aware of himself as being part of the creative process, or Tao, and is aware of this creative process within himself. Enlightenment does not mean that all mental activity ceases. What is meant by the phrase 'the ending of all thought' is that thought is no longer forced, that there is no division between thought and action, and that the mind no longer clings to any particular thought or thoughts but is open and responsive, a state of mind that issues in the unforced action of *wu-wei*. That Gunn thought about and understood this is clear from the notes he took from *The Secret of the Golden Flower*, particularly the following sentence: 'The secret of the magic of life consists in using action in order to attain non-

43

action.'[8] 'Non-action', of course, is the unforced action of *wu-wei*, which is described time and again in Gunn's novels, and which is glossed in the article 'Light' as 'complete relaxation, easy movements in freedom, and an amused foresight of how to deal successfully with all future events and encounters.'[9] This kind of action is only possible when man is in harmony with Tao, as it is a direct expression of the creative process itself. This is because the Tao is not a mere philosophical concept, but is quite simply and unequivocally the 'way' of nature. A contemporary Zen master has described the process of meditation in terms that highlight this connection:

> Stillness in the midst of action is the fundamental principle of *Zazen* (sitting in meditation). Some people think of *Zazen* as a sort of monopoly of the Zen sect, but the sect has no monopoly of it. *Zazen* is the basis of the universe. Heaven and earth sit in meditation, every object sits in meditation. Knowing nothing of the Zen sect, all things are performing their meditation.
>
> What is called *Zazen* means to live at peace in the true basis of the universe, which is stillness. Movement is a secondary attribution: stillness is the real condition. Out of stillness comes all activity.[10]

Awareness of this stillness comes from quietly watching the mind. In his *Saltire Review* article of 1958, 'The Flash', Gunn said it very simply: 'Keep silent and still and watch what happens.' And throughout *Highland River*, as we listen to Kenn's voice going over earlier events, and coming gradually to a full awareness of what he is *now*, this quietly responsive state of mind is much in evidence. In fact it is the characteristic tone of the whole book, and achieves its effect by creating in the reader a similar state of mind. Gunn takes the reader into the experience of meditation by allowing him access to the thought-patterns of a highly sensitive and intelligent mind. In reading *Highland River* one is not simply hearing Kenn's story passively, but becomes involved in a continual process of self-examination leading to a greater degree of self-awareness.

The process begins in Chapter 1, where the reader sees Kenn, as a boy, taking his first salmon. The whole episode, marvellously realised, shows how Kenn was first awakened to an awareness of another reality behind the surface of his life. The catching of the salmon symbolises Kenn's glimpse of the 'other landscape', and shows that Kenn is sufficiently mature not to lose control of himself in the face of such awareness. The choice of the salmon as a symbol of the elusive meaning of life is masterly. In part this comes from Gunn's manipulation of the Celtic myth of the 'salmon of wisdom', in much the same way as he was to do in later novels such as *The Green Isle of the Great Deep*. But much more it has to do with the actuality of the fish, and with Gunn's own precise observation of its nature. In a book about a Highland river a salmon could never appear out of place, but what Gunn achieves in this book is to show that precisely *this* natural creature in its own place is also intensely mysterious. The salmon has its undeniable symbolic function, but its ungraspableness is also its very reality: 'he was hunting nothing abstract. The "salmon of knowledge" for him had real silver scales and a desirable shape . . .' (p.288) And from the very beginning of *Highland River* the reader is drawn into contact with this same unpredictable and ungraspable reality as it impinges on the life of the young Kenn.

As in Joyce's *A Portrait of the Artist as a Young Man*, the opening of this novel plunges the reader right into the consciousness of its young protagonist. Here we see Kenn grudgingly carrying out the mundane daily chore of fetching water from the river. The very ordinariness of his reactions to having to wake up at six o'clock on a grey, frosty morning brings him close to the reader. He 'mumbles' and 'grumbles', and deliberately doesn't put on his boots so that his parents can see what a martyr he is, going out so early into the cold. In this same mood he carelessly bumps down the pail beside the river. And in that moment everything is changed irrevocably by the coming of the salmon.

The change that takes place with the ploughing of the salmon across the pool is a change not only in the world Kenn sees but also a change in the way he sees his own place in that world: 'When the waves faded out on the far side of the stream, where the bed was three feet deep, Kenn felt the great silence that lay upon the world and stood in the midst of it trembling like a

45

hunted hare.' (pp.10–11) This change affects both the physical and the metaphysical levels of reality. Kenn has been shocked into an awareness of things beyond himself, of things *in* himself which he cannot consciously control. The strangeness of this new feeling is conveyed through a powerful image of touch: 'Out of that noiseless world in the grey of the morning, all his ancestors came at him. They tapped his breast until the bird inside it fluttered madly; they drew a hand along his hair until the scalp crinkled . . .' (p.11) The image is archetypal; the interpretation of one level of reality or existence by another. Every reader knows consciously the 'sinking sensation', the weakness induced by panic fear, and is aware of the inter-connectedness of the physical and spiritual aspects of the human body. In *Totem and Taboo* Freud had drawn attention to man's primitive fear of being touched. And whether conscious or not the reader of *Highland River* experiences the same gut reaction to Gunn's image of Kenn's ancestors drawing a hand along his hair.

The strangeness of the whole episode is also suggested by a glimpse of Kenn as the salmon sees him, 'an altogether strange and ungainly beast . . . This rushing, sprawling, stone-throwing inhabitant of another world had fingers that slid off the back like caressing fingers of seaweed. Unable to bite yet pursuing relentlessly.' (p.15) This incident with the salmon shows many varied aspects of the boy, as if in an attempt to question the validity of any one particular view of his identity.

Among other things Kenn's fight with the salmon serves as an initiation into the masculine world of his father, and the other men of the village. And in that moment Kenn becomes part of the sexual polarity so characteristic of such a com-munity, evoked so vividly by his mother later in the book in terms of her own marriage:

> Yet her son was following the tradition of the men of her race . . .
> the thing was in the very warp and weft of their lives; one with the
> stormy seas; the dark winter mornings when her husband rose
> from her side and, with his heavy line on his oilskin back, shut the
> door behind him and left her listening to the ominous wind.
> (pp.291–2)

Entering this masculine world changes Kenn's relationship with the community as a whole. He is no longer a child, but is on the verge of manhood. The taking of the salmon would help ease the financial situation of his family, but more than that it is achieved by Kenn's taking upon himself the consciousness and the responsibilities of the hunter, the personal responsibility with which to challenge the uncertainties of water, the everchanging medium of his father's world.

In taking the salmon Kenn has chosen the path of his father, has chosen to cleave to the male traditions of the community, and thus must delineate taboo areas between himself and the female life of that community. In particular this emerges in the changed relationship between him and his mother, seen most clearly in the 'sort of manly reticence' with which he refuses to allow his mother to dry him after his soaking in the well pool. The same reticence is apparent also in the way in which his father is modest in his estimate of the weight of the salmon. Sans the shopkeeper says, 'He's hiding his pride fine', and Kenn's mother takes this to refer to Kenn himself although he could easily be talking of her husband, so proud of his son's courage and determination. The slight ambiguity serves to emphasise the link between father and son. It is Sans also who welcomes Kenn to the more boisterous side of male comrade-ship. 'When he saw the size of the fish, he muttered in astonishment a comical Gaelic oath, then laughed and brought down his hand on Kenn's shoulder. He shook Kenn. He stooped and looked into his eyes. "Good for you my little hero!" he chuckled.' (p.25) Sans' humour and bravado help to lighten the significance of the episode—an episode which for Kenn and his family is momentous. Never again will their relationship be quite the same. Each of them feels this, and the presence of Sans helps them to assimilate the change. Sans himself is keenly aware of this, is aware of the ritualistic nature of much of the conversation, and does much to lighten the solemnity of the occasion.

Kenn's father utters a quiet blessing in the awareness that Kenn is no longer simply a child, but is now alive to the complexities and mysteries of adult experience. In the same moment Kenn sees his father, and is likewise aware of their changed relationship:

> His father was a great and daring seaman; when he read the Bible and prayed he was a bearded patriarchal man; in danger his spirit flashed indomitable and challenging. Now his features softened in a slow winning smile, touched to the breath of wonder. His son felt it without looking at it, felt it in the breath of his voice, and a weakening warmth ran about his heart. (p.23)

His mother is also aware of the change that has come over her son, and it is interesting to see how her response to this develops through the episode. When Kenn takes the salmon back to the house his mother is immediately aware of the nature of the transformation that has taken place:

> She looked at the frightening size of the fish on the floor; she looked at her son. His dark hair was flattened to rat tails; his brown eyes were black against the excited pallor of his face; water seeped from his clothes; his body seemed no longer boyish but immature and fragile, his bones thin brittle stalks. Yet there was a flame, an intolerant fighting spirit, that knit him together, and separated him from her in a way that suddenly pulled at her heart. (p.22)

This is still her son, yet not her son. She senses immediately Kenn's discovery of his own individual identity as part of, yet separate from, herself. She is aware of the intense physical and mental effort required for him to catch the salmon and, through this, the degree to which Kenn had asserted that individuality. There is great poignancy in the picture of a mother who has just realised that her son no longer belongs to her in the old way, but belongs to himself and is a member of the community in his own right. She feels a mixture of sadness and pride, with not a little of the fear of growing old and useless.

Kenn, however, the hero of the well pool, is still a small boy who must rely on his parents for many things and at the time, the gift of a new pair of boots is as momentous to him as his catching of the salmon. There is really only a something in Kenn's eyes which marks the change. This is an awareness of vision and Kenn's eyes are referred to time and again throughout *Highland River* precisely because of this gleam of vision, of some latent quality within him. This is where the real significance of the episode lies in relation to the book as a whole. It is not simply that Kenn has caught the salmon, that he learned something specific from his experience, but that he has learned how to handle a potential for experience, for learning things from that experience. Through this encounter Kenn is awakened to a great capacity within himself for life in all its manifestations, and a respect for its mysteries.

The momentousness of the encounter lies in the extent to which it has highlighted the fact that his normal, egocentric attitude to reality is not enough—that somehow this kind of attitude filters out the 'suchness' of the world in favour of more easily assimilable ideas about it. The appearance of the salmon forces Kenn to go beyond this habitually blinkered view of reality, and engage more directly with the world. Fear gives way to exaltation as he learns how to handle this increased awareness, and this whole inner movement is conveyed to the reader by Gunn's close observation of Kenn's physical and mental responses to the twisting flashing unknown of the salmon.

This abrupt increase in responsiveness is precisely the *satori* of Zen:

> The essence of Zen Buddhism consists in acquiring a new viewpoint of looking at life and things generally . . . Zen . . . assures us of the acquirement of a new point of view in which life assumes a fresher, deeper, and more satisfying aspect. This acquirement, however, is really and naturally the greatest mental cataclysm one can go through with in life.[11]

And in making this shift Kenn comes face to face with what Gunn was later to term his 'second self'—that part of an individual which is beyond the accidentals of any particular social system, and which is part of Tao. In *The Atom of Delight* Gunn points out that however difficult it may be to describe the experience of coming upon this area of one's personality there can be no denying the actuality of it when it happens:

> In brief, as the self is borne away, as the central ego or clot thins, so is the self more profoundly and centrally enriched. This is a

common experience. It happens. The wording, the analogy, may be matter for debate. There is no doubt about the happening, about the feeling, the apprehension, that in those minutes one was with one's real self, and also with that which was beyond the real self but yet of which the real self was part. (p.237)

And in a letter to Professor Nakamura, Gunn described the second self succinctly:

In that extraordinary moment when one becomes aware of oneself, self-aware, it is exactly as if there was an over-self seeing the ordinary self, and this creates a sort of amplitude of being in which there is light, and delight, and understanding. The 'first self' and the 'second self' (or, above, the ordinary and the over-self) are now one, the second containing the first within its circle, which can—and generally does—expand outwards with a wonderful sense of freedom, or may narrow upon the first self with an understanding that has its own clear affection, a seeing that comprehends the whole, the unity and accepts within a—or the—region of ultimate Reality.[12]

Coming upon the second self one is aware of 'an amplitude of being', the expansive feeling of joy, of delight. And this is also evident in Kenn's case. In coming upon his second self, Kenn is transformed, and the fight with the salmon is carried out in a state of heightened awareness. All his energy is focussed in the attempt to capture the magical creature. His attention is not fixed on any one plan of attack, but is relaxed and open, leaving himself room to respond to the unexpected. Involved in such intense activity success will only come if both body and mind can remain light and responsive. For Gunn one of the most potent images of this kind of awareness was the figure of the Japanese Zen archer as portrayed in Herrigel's *Zen in the Art of Archery*. He devoted a central chapter in *The Atom of Delight* to giving an account both of Herrigel's book and of the archer's central dilemma of having to learn to stop consciously controlling his weapon so as to let control happen 'of itself':

The rest of the book describes with an engaging lucidity the long and arduous struggle towards mastery of a bow and arrow. For, to begin with, the bow was over six feet long and to draw it the full length of the arrow and hold it before letting go required such muscular exertion and tension, with labouring of breath, that in the ordinary way it was quite a physical feat. Once more consider the pupil's astonishment when he was told that there must be no such muscular tension and labouring of breath; that in fact the muscles of his arms and shoulders should remain loose and relaxed; the hand must do it all, and almost as if it weren't doing it at that. (pp.135–6)

Indeed the martial arts have long been connected with Zen in Japan, where it is fully understood that the way of Zen is not concerned purely with the mental aspects of a person's life, but is a path that necessitates a total integration of one's mental and physical capabilities in the effort to break through to Enlightenment. But the active, *yang*, side of Zen is always tempered by its passive or *yin* aspect, resulting in a mode of action that is never wild and erratic but always quietly controlled and responsive to any change in circumstances:

'What is most important in the art of fencing is to acquire a certain mental attitude known as "immovable wisdom" . . . "Immovable" does not mean to be stiff and heavy and lifeless as a rock or a piece of wood. It means the highest degree of motility with a centre which remains immovable. The mind then reaches the highest point of alacrity ready to direct its attention anywhere it is needed—to the left, to the right, to all the directions as required . . .

This—what may be termed the "non-interfering" attitude of mind—constitutes the most vital element in the art of fencing as well as in Zen.'[13]

In taking the salmon Kenn displays precisely this kind of awareness. The attention must never be forced, but must be allowed to follow the changing nature of reality lightly. The reality may be general or specific. Lao Tsu said that one must rule a kingdom as one cooks a small fish—'lightly'; too much interference will hinder the possibility of success. And in *Highland River* 'reality' for the younger Kenn is the salmon, while for Kenn the physicist, engaged in his quest for the source, 'reality' is his past. Both of them learn by experience the truth of Lao Tsu's adage; both of them learn to handle reality 'lightly'.

51

And the river itself is instrumental in the development of this capacity, as Gunn shows in his treatment of the relationship between Kenn and his brother Angus. For Kenn the river is clearly part of him, a fact of which he is fully aware: 'From that day the river became the river of life for Kenn . . . In zero moments it could rise before him with the clearness of a chart showing the main current of his nervous system and its principal tributaries.' (p.54) The interpenetration of Kenn and the river is made even more concrete in two images where Kenn listens to the sound of the river and discovers this to be the sound of his own heart: 'Contract and expand, systole and diastole: the river flows . . . (p.148) Faintly he heard the surge of the stream away underground. So it was not lost! But listening more acutely, he realised that what he heard was the surge of the river of his own blood.' (p.343) Such images convey powerfully to the reader Kenn's sense of the river as his sustaining life-force.

The river is also the river of life of the community and symbolises for Kenn all the positive values of that community. As his superior, Radzyn the Polish scientist, points out, Kenn's personal vision is wedded insolubly to the traditions of his people; 'You have the folk idea strong in you'. It is this connection with the river that ensures that Kenn's life is 'charmed'. Throughout Chapter 3, which deals with his wartime experiences, his survival and his success as a soldier are directly linked to his vision of the river, his awareness of what it represents. Even after being temporarily blinded by gas on the Somme, Kenn's inner vision of the river proves to be a sustaining force. Regaining consciousness in hospital he hears again the flowing of the river. 'He had been deaf for a long time, but was now listening acutely, he could hear the rumble of the hospital noises like the far cry of brown water in the hollow of a strath.' (p.65)

And when Kenn later encounters Angus in the trenches it is clear that Angus has done his best to forget about the river, so that whenever Kenn tries to make him remember it is like touching a raw nerve:

> And once Angus looked about him with a sudden start as if in the
> short absence of thought something might have crept nearer. For

there was no reality in the river. There was no reality outside the world in which he was. And the wariness and cuteness served merely to emphasise how inevitable and unending was its maze, with the trapped mind doomed to dodge about for ever. (p.228)

Encountering this new Angus, whose spirit is broken, the reader recalls the darker undertones of a poaching trip Kenn and Angus had made as children and described by Gunn in Chapter 12. On that occasion Angus was to initiate his younger brother into a knowledge of the higher reaches of the river, and Kenn's excitement at this is evident. Set amid Gunn's beautiful and exact evocation of the natural world the episode describes the attempts of Kenn and Angus to catch a salmon. Kenn learns much from Angus who, after several attempts does land a salmon. On their way home the boys narrowly avoid being discovered by the keepers, but on the whole they feel it has been quite a successful day.

Yet there is a darker side to this chapter. Three times Angus fails to take a salmon and the reader immediately recalls the certainty with which Kenn had taken his salmon in the book's opening episode. The implication is that Kenn, in catching the salmon of widom has assimilated some of its magical power while Angus, through this failure to catch the fish, renounces his right to that power. And as he misses the salmon his face darkens and his expression becomes clouded, qualities symbolising his denial of the light, his lack of spiritual vision. On one occasion he loses his temper and swears at Kenn:

> Kenn felt the attack bitterly. It was a dark, horrible moment, a pit in which the brightness of the day vanished, in which their lovely friendship was smothered.
>
> Angus's fists were tight-clenched. He looked away. 'God damn it!' he said.
>
> Very rarely did the boys of that river swear. 'A dirty mouth' was a reproach amongst them, and a grown man at sound of even an ambiguous oath would quickly enough warm a cheek. Angus's expression was thus like the going out of the sun. (pp.207–8)

The contrast between the two brothers is seen also in their attitudes to the community which had nurtured them:

'I saw in a book about the Celtic people', said Kenn, 'they were people somewhere in the olden times. I forget what it was all about, except two lines, and they were something about "the hazel nuts of knowledge and the salmon of wisdom". It made me think of the strath. Funny, wasn't it?'

'Not much sense in it.'

'No,' said Kenn at once. 'Only I thought it was queer at the time.'

'They believed anything in the olden times.'

'Yes,' said Kenn. (p.203)

This brief scrap of conversation economically highlights the difference between Kenn and his brother. The tentativeness of Kenn's observations gives Angus a lead to open up the conversation, but he is not sufficiently responsive to the situation to see this, and his short replies clearly convey his unwillingness even to consider doing so. This lack of responsiveness extends also to the community of which he is part. Angus here shows what he thinks of the community which sustains him. The 'river of life' and the 'salmon of wisdom' have a living reality for Kenn, but to Angus they are mere superstition. This difference of faith is in the end the difference between life and death for the two brothers. Kenn's life *is* 'charmed', because of his highly responsive attitude to the world, an attitude which is centred in that creative field of which the individual human life is but one aspect. Angus has denied this insight, and the denial costs him his life.

And ultimately the whole of Neil Gunn's fiction is about life, about the actual experience of living. For, as he wrote in *The Atom of Delight*:

> For it is here in the coming upon the second self that freedom and choice operate as elements of a living whole, of a livingness that is the creative entity, and as such are inseparable from the act of being alive and thus beyond logical analysis, as life is beyond it. (p.246)

The theorising, the investigation of the significance of delight, is as nothing compared to the actuality of the experience itself. This is why at the end of the book Gunn does not *tell* us the meaning of Kenn's reaching the source of his river. Instead he concentrates on subtly evoking something of the movement of Kenn's mind up to his final vision.

Kenn's quest for the source is a journey back in time, from the contemporary civilisation of his village at the mouth of the river, through the ancient domain of the Picts, to the immeasurable time beyond. But Gunn clearly does not want us to see this as a regressive movement. There is something positive in this quest back to the primitive and beyond. And this positive is the liberation of the mind from its domination by analytical thought. Gunn does not advocate a turning away from thought altogether, but he is so aware of the limiting nature of the uncontrolled intellect that he sees man as trapped by a faculty which should be one of his greatest assets. In *The Shadow*, Nan puts it thus: 'We have to rescue the intellect from the destroyers. They have turned it into death rays and it should be the sun.' (p.42) When thought becomes reductive, as analytical thought so often and so easily does, then it becomes destructive. Thus a prominent motif in *Highland River* concerns the delight experienced when the restrictions of thought fall away and the human being acts spontaneously and intuitively. In the first chapter Kenn is startled out of his habitual thought patterns by the coming of the salmon. The wartime contrast between Kenn and Angus shows how Kenn, light and intuitive, survives while Angus, who has dwelt too much on the dangers of his situation, is killed.

It should come as no surprise, then, to find that one of the most important aspects of Kenn's final vision on the moor in the last chapter of *Highland River* is that conscious thought in its reductive, analytical form falls away from him. This happens naturally, 'of itself', as Kenn sits down to eat his sandwiches:

> He had nothing to drink, so chewed away at the sandwiches as he stared at the water at his feet, until the mood of communion with the sodden black earth—too often an imagined mood—became a mindless reality, with physical points of discomfort where the sweat was drying to a chill in the small of his back and the rain was wetting a knee and a shoulder. But he could not be bothered shifting the knee or the shoulder. Once his eyes glimmered in the

humour that might have said, 'This is fine,' but his lips remained soundless and the glimmer passed. (pp.336–7)

This 'communion with the sodden black earth' of the moor recalls a similar moment in *Butcher's Broom*, where Elie finds her own inner strength by experiencing this absolute selflessness. Here Kenn's awareness is quieter, but the significance of the experience is the same. It is the awareness of meditation in which Kenn is quietly aware without letting his thoughts interfere with that awareness. This is the state of no-mind (*wu-hsin*) in which all concern for 'self' disappears; although Kenn is fully aware of the various points of physical discomfort he makes no attempt to get rid of them, and this state of poised awareness is the experience of delight described so perfectly by Te-shan: 'Only when you have no thing in your mind and no mind in things are you vacant and spiritual, empty and marvellous.'[14] Thought and the idea of self conjured up by thought fall away from Kenn who is now in communion with his second self, is aware of himself as part of a larger unity, no longer separated from the world around him.

This is conveyed to the reader in the very next paragraph. Kenn stirs the pool of water at his feet with his stick, thus recalling a similar occasion in Chapter 11, where he had done likewise. From the juxtaposition of these two separate and yet identical Kenns, the reader's own sense of self is jolted and redefined:

> The small pool in the black peat at his feet became a world of its own. It was separated from the stream by a green bank. The reflections of the rushes seemed more vivid than the rushes themselves, more intricate in their patterns. The end of his hazel crook stirred the pool and bubbles came to life on its surface. The bubbles had an attraction for one another. When two grew close together they rushed into a violent embrace and became one. The one sailed about for a time, then burst, and from the place where it had been went out an uncountable number of close concentric waves, as if the skin of the pool shivered. Idly the stick created more individual bubbles. They united; they died. Some never united. But they all died. (p.337)

The pool at Kenn's feet is a microcosmic world in which bubbles appear bearing an anthropomorphic relation to human beings. They 'come to life', 'have an attraction for one another', they pair off, 'draw close together', and 'rush into a violent embrace and become one'; they survive a little and then die. This is Eliot's world of birth, copulation and death, a rather bleak vision of humanity. But from Kenn's new perspective what becomes apparent is the fact that, however arbitrary the creation of the bubbles which are individual consciousness, there *are* always bubbles, and furthermore the bubbles of individual consciousness are part of a larger field of consciousness. And this is the fundamental insight of Buddhism:

> The basic teaching of Buddhism is the teaching of transciency, or change. That everything changes is the basic truth for each existence . . . This teaching is also understood as the teaching of selflessness. Because each existence is in constant change, there is no abiding self.[15]

In this relation of the individual consciousness to the larger field of consciousness lies the significance of *Highland River*. Kenn's quest for self-knowledge takes him beyond the accidents of the ego, of the social personality, to a direct intuitive awareness of his second self, of what Zen Buddhists would call his 'original face'. This is possible because the second self is part of the larger creative field of Tao. In his *Zen Doctrine of No Mind*, D. T. Suzuki quotes Zen's Sixth Patriarch, Hui-neng: 'There is within oneself that which knows, and thereby one has a *satori*.'[16] And Gunn himself drew attention to this property of the second self in *The Atom of Delight*: 'The second self is not an assumption. It is the fount from which assumptions proceed. In the beginning it is. I am itself, trying to describe it.'[17]

Kenn the boy and Kenn the physicist are equally unreal, and yet somewhere along the line that unites and divides them there is an essential Kenn, a Kenn who is not to be identified with either role, but which is the common ground between them. The vision in the peat pool reflects something of Kenn's new awareness of the self not as something fixed and static, but as something closer to the Eastern concept of self based on change and relativity and with the individual self seen as part of a larger process. Suzuki quotes Bodhidharma on this in his first series of *Essays:*

> The Buddha is your own Mind, make no mistake to bow [to external objects]. 'Buddha' . . . means 'enlightened nature'; and by 'enlightened nature' is meant 'spiritually enlightened'. It is one's own spiritual Nature in enlightenment that responds to the external world, comes in contact with objects, raises the eyebrows, winks the eyelids, and moves the hands and legs. This Nature is the Mind, and the Mind is the Buddha, and the Buddha is the Way, and the Way is Zen . . . To see directly into one's original Nature, this is Zen.[18]

As conscious thought falls away from Kenn on the moor he becomes aware of the world in a more creative way, becoming aware of some of its symbolic significance. He catches a glimpse of some hinds which are part of that stratum of the book's imagery concerning magical beasts such as the salmon and the green linnet, so the reader is quite prepared for the shift on to the other landscape where the hinds are at once a natural part of the landscape and a vision of human possibility. Yet even if the reader is unaware of this Gunn describes beautifully the fading away of the deer as of a vision:

> As he broke out of this mood, the farthest hind trotted a few steps, then turned its head again in that high flat-browed ear-pointed look that has something memoried about it out of some leprechaun world. The other two trotted and looked. More heads were lifted. Movement began in hesitant starts and pauses; rhythms taken up and broken, yet ever running together. The last to see him was a mother hind with her calf beside her. She wheeled round and was off, but holding herself in, too, her head thrown back, and riding above her body with a lovely grace. He looked for the others. They were gone. The calf was pale against the golden tan of its mother and ran eagerly at its mother's side. In no time they were gone also. In the soft ground there had been no sound of hooves. There had indeed been no sound at all. (p.340)

This is accurate naturalistic description but is at the same time open-ended and highly-suggestive symbolism, in which the total soundlessness of the experience adds to its visionary quality.

On the moor, then, Kenn's experience is reverberant with meaning. Internal and external continually merge as suggested to the reader by the constant interaction of symbol and reality. Kenn's experiences on the moor are also experiences in some austere region of his mind. After seeing the deer Kenn's mind is drawn to two boats whose names are *Aristocratic* and *Thoroughbred*, the memorable qualities he had recognised in the appearance of the deer. They are also the special qualities of the fishermen, men like Kenn's own father, and Kenn is aware of how these qualities have been degraded by 'the whole historic social process', which has always tended to ignore man's closeness to nature and to set man apart thus cutting him off from his roots and taking away his dignity. The dignity and breadth of the fishermen comes from the preservation of this essential link to something greater than man's own self-enclosed vision of the world. In an image which recalls his capture of the 'salmon of wisdom' Kenn realises the necessity of preserving this link. 'When the spirit of man recaptured the grace of the hinds, the two words would once more have meaning. Not until then.' (p.341)

By the simple device of portraying Kenn's thoughts, 'hesitant and swift as a herd of hinds', Gunn draws the seemingly disparate elements of his novel together. The reader should try not to come to any conclusions, but should try to glimpse the relationships between the various parts. The futility of forming conclusions is brought home to Kenn himself when he sees his stream vanish into the earth.

> His dismay was vague and ludicrous. From his map-gazing he knew that his river should rise in a loch. He could not have been mistaken. This loch was to have been the end of his journey. Like the Yogi in his pilgrimage to Lake Manas!
>
> And here it was coming out of the earth itself. The realism mocked him. He had actually thought of a loch with shores of sand and water grey in the evening light.
>
> Coming out of a black hole in the earth like life itself. A hole that was like death. Life and death in ooze. He poked into the dark hole with his stick. (pp.342–3)

Again the image of Kenn with his stick, poking about in the ooze, seeking an answer. And this time the answer comes as he hears the surge of the stream underground. But the sound of the water is really 'the surge of the river of his own blood'. On realising this Kenn is able to go on to discover the actual loch: 'its shores were not of dove-grey sand but of pure ground quartz, paler than any woman's face in any old poet's dream.' (p.344) At this loch Kenn discovers the delicate hoof-marks of the hinds that come here to drink. This is the source that sustains the magical beasts.

Kenn remains there, still hoping to have a vision, until he realises that only human vanity wishes to have visions, and as he realises his essential loneliness he begins to understand how this is reflected in the traditions of his people:

> He saw its meaning in his people, even in their religion, for what was the Calvinist but one who would have no mediating figure between himself and the Ultimate, no one to take responsibility from him, to suffer for him. (p.345)

Kenn's mother and father are evoked in that paragraph, just as Kenn himself figures largely in the next which connects the scientist's search for truth with poaching forays and a quest for a water-head. In wrestling with this complex of identities and roles, as he had wrestled with the salmon in Chapter 1, Kenn moves to a greater self-awareness: not an awareness of Kenn as boy, physicist, or as son, but the central consciousness which is all of these simultaneously.

> The gathering clot of moody denial dissolved like tiredness from his flesh, and his body lay to the sands lightly in a desire for sleep. As his eyes looked across the water, they smiled. Out of great works of art, out of great writing, there comes upon the soul sometimes a feeling of strange intimacy. It is the moment in which all conflict is reconciled, in which a timeless harmony is achieved.
>
> It was coming upon him now. (p.346)

In the acuteness of Kenn's vision the inessentials have faded out, leaving him, as Sandy puts it in *Bloodhunt*, 'at the heart of what seemed like the creative intention'. And in *The Atom of Delight* Gunn writes:

Nothing is any more except what is now, and what is now has been called light, love, harmony, integration, participation in the all or the absolute; indeed many variations and combinations of such terms have been used by those who, having had this experience, have wished to communicate it, to share it. But although the actual experience cannot be communicated to those who have never had it, yet there seems to be something apprehensible in the way, or along the path, of the happening or experience that can, however vaguely or informally, be caught by all.[19]

Indeed it is a characteristic of the experience of Enlightenment that it is beyond the reach of words and of conceptual thought, as Suzuki points out in the first series of *Essays:*

Satori is the most intimate individual experience and therefore cannot be expressed in words or described in any manner. All that one can do in the way of communicating the experience to others is to suggest or indicate, and this only tentatively.[20]

In *Highland River* the suggestions and indications come through the reader's involvement in Kenn's thought-patterns, until the mind is stilled along with Kenn's so that the silence at the end of the journey is fully comprehended. To ask for explicitness at the end of *Highland River* is to have missed both the experience and the meaning. The humour of such a situation would not have been lost on Gunn:

I have read somewhere a story of Chinese who trekked across Asian country to receive, by order of Buddha, a copy of the scriptures. On opening their copy they found that it contained no writing. When they showed Buddha the blank pages, he smiled. They were wanting it in writing even then.[21]

THE HEART OF THE CIRCLE
The Silver Darlings 1941

The growth of self-knowledge, as portrayed by Gunn in *Highland River*, can be achieved with little obvious sense of strain. But this is not always the case, and *The Silver Darlings* (1941) is an exploration of the painful struggle of its central characters to self-awareness. The book was written during a time of conflict and anxiety in Gunn's personal life which seems to have been resolved with the outbreak of the Second World War, and with a recognition of his vocation as a writer, a recognition possibly precipitated by the writing of *The Silver Darlings* itself. Two diary entries from this time give some indication of his state of mind. The first, on 3 September 1939, describes his immediate response to the radio newscast informing the British people of the outbreak of war. 'The mind can't make much of it. The body feels tired, exhausted. One can do little but stare at the thought of war, with its fugitive hellish pictures of destruction.'[1] An entry the following day shows how the public crisis of the war brought into focus some of the private doubts and conflicts which were troubling him:

> Again I feel that if I went back to work, I should probably stop writing. To a man of my age, this war is going to be a critical period. It will be a period during which anything creative will have every chance of being quietly smothered. Not that I expect anything much from myself. But in these last two years or so I have been increasingly conscious of certain qualities like light and happiness, conscious of them in a triple aspect—personal, philosophic, and artistic. I might, if left to myself to ponder on

63

them, manage to produce or reproduce them in writing. I know that if I could do this, it would be a vastly greater service to some of my fellows than would any routine clerical job in a service department. I am convinced, further, that writers will have to do something like this, in the first place to save the integrity of the individual threatened by the tyranny of the mass or collective-mass, and in the second, to revitalise the core of life itself in each individual. These are vague words, but I know what I mean . . .[2]

It is pertinent also that *The Silver Darlings* is dedicated to the memory of Gunn's father, a fisherman. On its most obvious level the book is a hymn of praise to the fishermen of Caithness; men whom Gunn had already praised in *Highland River* for their dignity and breadth of character, qualities he saw as stemming directly from their relationship with the sea: 'cleanness and precision of action, arose necessarily from the traffic with the sea. They were the only qualities that could hope to counter the impersonal fury, the impending, curling-over, smashing destruction of the sea.'[3]

Throughout Gunn's fiction the fisherman is a symbol of balance and integrity. This is nowhere more so than in *The Silver Darlings*, written shortly after Gunn's own encounter with the sea when he and his wife sailed round Scotland's west coast, a journey described in *Off in a Boat*. It seems that at this time Gunn might have been regretting the fact that he had not followed the sea like his father. A sentence tucked away near the end of *Highland River* carries something of this sense of inadequacy:

> Davy's secret hope had been placed in his son Angus, but Angus had gone with other lads to Canada four years before, and so the tradition of the sea was broken. This was a hidden source of regret for him; but outwardly he recognised the stress of circumstance.[4]

Other factors, such as the central tangled relationship of Finn, his mother Catrine, Tormad his dead father, and Roddie, the father-figure who eventually marries Catrine, point to the personal nature of much of the exploration in *The Silver Darlings*. It was a book Gunn did not enjoy writing, but it is probably his most finished and his most mature book, in the sense of dealing fully with adult relationships with a psychological insight which penetrates beyond the intellect to the actual living quality of the various relationships involved.

Underlying all the human relationships of *The Silver Darlings* is the presence of the sea:

> They had never before been so far from land, and the slow movement of the sea became a living motion under them. It brimmed up against the boat and choked its own mouth, then moved away; and came again and moved away, without end, slow, heedless, and terrible, its power restrained, like the power in some great invisible bull. Fear, feather light, kept them wary, like the expectancy of a blow in a dark place. (p.17)

The fear, like the fear of darkness, is primal. It is man's fear of that which he cannot consciously control, a reality greater than himself. The sea in *The Silver Darlings* is a symbol of the unconscious.

This world beyond the influence of conscious will is the great void which underlies all human action.

> Something mysteriously formed,
> Born before heaven and earth.
> In the silence and the void,
> Standing alone and unchanging,
> Ever present and in motion.
> Perhaps it is the mother of ten thousand things.
> I do not know its name.
> Call it Tao.
> For lack of a better name, I call it great.[5]

In the great void a man can, if he perseveres, come to an awareness of a greater reality—the second self. If he is capable of this then the void is seen as liberating, but for many people the world beyond the limitations of the conscious ego is a world of fear and pain. This is so precisely because they *do* cling so tightly to the security of the ego. The sea, representing the void, lies behind all the changing human relationships of *The Silver Darlings* as the standard by which we must judge the growth of the human characters.

This is clear right from the opening chapter of the book which gives an account of the people's first attempt at fishing. 'From time immemorial' this people had lived on the land, and their whole culture and way of life was intimately bound up with that land; a fact Gunn had impressed strongly on his readers through the figure of Dark Mairi in *Butcher's Broom*. The opening of *The Silver Darlings* emphasises how difficult had been the change from a land-based economy to life on the shore: 'That first winter had been a terror. For one long spell, they had had little or nothing to live on but shell-fish and seaweed. Often they ate the wrong thing and colic and dysentery were everywhere.' (p.13)

'Often they ate the wrong thing.' The people are no longer in their natural element. Everything here on the shore is strange to them. In *Butcher's Broom* Dark Mairi represents, among other things, a traditional way of life which, because of long and intimate knowledge of one place, was capable of maintaining a balanced existence in that place. Mairi, with her knowledge of the natural world would have known what could be eaten safely. With the death of Mairi, and of others like her, during the Clearances, this continuity of knowledge had been broken, and with it the possibility of a balanced existence. That crucial connection with a sustaining 'source' has been lost.

The Silver Darlings charts the people's attempts to regain something of that balance, and so an awareness of the Clearances lies behind much of the action. It is stressed in this first account of the men putting out to sea. Making their way down to the shore they are watched, silently and expectantly, by the rest of the community. And when they do at last put to sea it is with trepidation and uncertainty. Their uncertainty of the sea is seen in Tormad's nervousness when a small wave splashes his feet, in Torquil's sea-sickness, and in their anxiety at being so far from the known world of the land. These small incidents remind us in a very concrete way that all this is a very new experience to the people involved. More pointed reference to the Clearances is made when the crew sight the strange ship that is to prove so hostile. 'Fear touched them once more, because they had learned that everything that spoke of power and wealth had to be feared. . . . "Pay no attention," muttered Tormad. "The sea at least is free." ' (p.27)

The brooding presence of the Clearances was even stronger in an earlier draft of this chapter which appeared in *The Scots Magazine* in December 1937 as 'The Boat'. One of the major differences between the two published versions is in a toning down of the references to the Clearances, which in 'The Boat' had been on a very polemical level, and a more careful concentration on evoking the strangeness of the sea itself to those involved, through the presentation of their own immediate responses to it—all those slight involuntary nervousnesses attending a new and possibly hazardous experience.

It is precisely this encounter with the void that is the subject of *The Silver Darlings*. The sea is seen as a 'heaving immensity, treacherous and deep as death' and the encounter with its sheer unknowability engenders tensions in all the human relationships in the book. This is clear from the outset, where we see Tormad taking his leave of Catrine to set off on that first fishing expedition. As Tormad prepares to go, Catrine is unable to preserve her calm and creates a 'scene', imploring him to stay. Although she is only nineteen she loves Tormad with a knowingness and intensity that belies her youth. Tormad, at twenty-four, is disturbed by his glimpse of love's intensity. 'He knew her wayward moods. But this was something far beyond. It was hard and challenging, without any warmth. Her eyes were suddenly those of an enemy, deliberately calculating, cold as greed.' (p.11) The innocence of their love has been darkened by Tormad's going to sea, by his assertion of a self separate from Catrine, and so her fear of the sea is more than a fear of the unknown element. It is a fear of Tormad's leaving her, of his developing a state of mind in which he will no longer need either her or her love. The insight is the woman's. Almost always in Gunn it is the women who *see* with such clarity just what is happening; Kenn's mother in *Highland River*, Elie in *Butcher's Broom*, and later Fand in *The Well at the World's End*. In *The Silver Darlings* the prospect of losing Tormad appears to Catrine with a devastating starkness. And yet this is perhaps to bring too sharp a focus to bear on something glimpsed and understood only obscurely. Tormad does not *want* to leave Catrine, and she in her turn does not *want* to love him so possessively. In the natural way of things both of them are developing emotionally, and they are both moving towards a greater individual fulfilment, and yet towards a deepening of their relationship with each other. As life is never static, but is constantly changing, it cannot be expected that this movement will be free of conflicts and anxieties. Conflict indeed is part of the process, and the anxieties are temporary.

In presenting such a confrontation right at the beginning of the novel, Gunn sets in train the subtle psychological probing that makes *The Silver Darlings* such a great novel. In this central relationship Gunn highlights immediately the archetypal nature of the encounter with the essential 'otherness' of the world beyond the limited perception of the ego that is the book's main theme. As in *Highland River*, reading becomes not a passive acquiescence with what is enacted in the pages of the novel, but rather a full involvement in the perceptions of human beings engaged in the struggle for self-knowledge.

From the outset, *The Silver Darlings* can be seen to explore the relationship between sexual awareness and self-knowledge. The initial tension between Catrine and Tormad is prophetic, as the two are indeed separated. While on the sea engaged in that first difficult search for fish Tormad and his crew are press-ganged, and Tormad himself dies shortly afterwards from injuries sustained during his capture. Catrine, after her initial despair, moves to Dunster where she attempts to start her life anew, living in the house of an old friend, the solid and reliable Kirsty Mackay ('Folk have to eat though the heavens fall'). Here, her son, Finn is born. From the beginning her life in Dunster is connected with that of Roddie Sinclair, skipper of a local fishing-boat; a man who at one point claims he is married to the sea. Roddie gradually becomes a father-figure to the young Finn who regards him in an heroic light, living as he does in close contact with the dangers and uncertainties of the sea. Roddie is also drawn to Catrine, and the novel is very much concerned with the psychological implications of this tangled relationship, with the development and change apparent in each of the characters' perception of the others. And, as Catrine understands from the beginning, the void which confronts them is most apparent in relationships between male and female. This knowledge comes to her in a disturbing dream:

> She was naturally afraid lest her very fear of having this dream would only help its recurrence and, growing accustomed to it, she might lose the strength to fight successfully. Deeper than that, too, was the awful suggestion she had got of the body's possible treachery and, far below that, of the horrible dark ultimate compliance of a mind that was hardly hers. (p.108)

For the unprepared, the encounter with the void is disturbing as it so undermines the security of ego-consciousness. Gunn's awareness of this was outlined in the article 'Highland Space', which appeared in *The Saltire Review* in 1961:

> There is the story of the man who after the last war (he had done most of his fighting in the desert) came back to his house, a croft between mountains, and stood the austerity for three days and nights, and then beat it. The mountains had got on top of him, the silence, the loneliness.[6]

What is fundamental, says Gunn, is the fear of empty space, and this is precisely because to recognise the essential emptiness of the outer world is to see with stark clarity the emptiness of the subjective ego. And yet, as he goes on to say in the same article, there is a different way of looking at this—a way that regards this emptiness as the creative source itself:

> . . . apparently our fear of space, the *horror vacui*, is not a fear in Zen, which uses words like Emptiness, Nothing, the Void, quite commonly, but always in the paradoxical sense that Emptiness is not emptiness, space is not Void, yet again, that they are these in the moment before they are not.[7]

One can see the void in this way only when one is Enlightened, and untroubled by the loss of the old sense of self. This is the insight of *satori*, and though instantaneous, the insight comes only to the mind which is ready for it. The road to wisdom is long and arduous. The action of *The Silver Darlings* charts the ups and downs of the journeys of its central characters: Tormad's first ill-fated venture on the sea, Catrine's journey into the strange new country of Caithness, Finn's journey to Wick in search of the plague doctor, Finn and Roddie's fishing voyages, and Finn's daring climb up the cliff-face to find food and water for his companions.

All of these can be seen as symbols of man's quest for awareness and fulfilment, but gradually the novel begins to focus on one particular journey—Finn's 'journey' from childhood, through rebellious adolescence, to maturity. This is paralleled in the growth of the herring industry, and in the people's growing self-confidence. This is the archetypal journey made by each of us in the ordinary course of our lives, and it is here that the 'legendary' world of *The Silver Darlings* connects most strongly with the lives of its readers, lifting its significance out of its historical setting and into the reader's immediate present.

Alexander Scott has pointed out that *The Silver Darlings*, along with *Morning Tide* and *Highland River*, are 'novels of initiation'. For their central characters, these are novels of initiation into the male, adult traditions of their community. They mark the transition from being a dependent, to becoming a fully-involved working member of the community. Beyond this they show the development of a fully individual personality. And beyond this they show how full development and maturity only come when a man can retain his own individuality while losing his selfishness. Within the circle of his own experience each person has to find his own place, a position in which he is perfectly balanced, and from which he can move freely without encroaching on other members of the community. This is to become 'centred' in the *mandala*, to have reached the source, to have passed beyond the ego to the second self, and to have found a proper balance between the inner and outer worlds.

In *The Silver Darlings*, Finn must go through this process of centring—a recognised description of the process of meditation. Indeed, that section of *Zen Flesh, Zen Bones* to which Neil Gunn most warmly responded, and which describes '112 ways to open the invisible door of consciousness', was properly entitled 'Centreing'. In Finn's case this involves not the conscious following of any particular 'Way', but rather the gradual

70

realisation that in all he does he *is* following a Way, and that this is simply the great Way of Tao. Yet this understanding does not come easily. As the circle of his experience widens in the natural process of growing up, Finn's personality develops accordingly and he bases his actions more and more in the accumulated aspects of his personality, not that second self which lies at the centre of all the additions. Because of this his actions are often erratic—the heroic scaling of the cliff-face, for instance, is partly an attack on Roddie, his rival for Catrine. The movement of the book shows how Finn is able to regain contact with the second self, and make his actions once again balanced and natural; fully in accord with the spontaneity (*tzu-jan*) of Tao.

This spontaneity and naturalness he has lost by his ego's refusal to acknowledge other facets of his personality. This denial of wholeness has meant that Finn's grasp of life is fragmented—a fragmentation that leads to erratic, unbalanced behaviour. And the refusal to acknowledge *all* aspects of his personality is caused quite simply by fear of the unknown—of the void. It is the panic fear which attacked Kenn at the beginning of *Highland River*, when the salmon first ploughed across the pool. But it is a fear that can be ended by fully understanding the reasons for it. Yet this is not the understanding of logical thought processes. Rather it is the direct insight of *prajñā*. Only when the whole being is involved rather than the partial aspect of logic, can such fear be allayed and the blocks to spontaneity removed. This involves nothing more esoteric than facing up to one's own weaknesses and blind-spots. And this is why some early Zen masters were so vehement in their condemnation of meditation as a conscious discipline—too often this can end in self-deception. In our own day the same point is made by Krishnamurti:

> Meditation is one of the most important things in life; not how to meditate; not meditation according to a system; not the practice of meditation; but rather that which meditation is.
>
> To see what one actually is, it is vital that there be freedom, freedom from the whole content of one's consciousness, the content of consciousness being all the things put together by

71

thought. Freedom from the content of one's consciousness, from one's angers and brutalities, from one's vanities and arrogance, from all the things that one is caught up in, is meditation.[9]

This means that the recognition of the reality of one's own present situation is itself the beginning of the insight of meditation.

Often this is a recognition of the darker side of one's character, which leads initially to a feeling of being trapped in a situation where retreat seems as dangerous as going on. This is the 'doubt sensation' which is a necessary precondition for the experience of *satori*:

When not spurred, no awakening;
When not cornered, no opening through.[10]

Finn is cornered by his refusal to acknowledge the relationship between Roddie and his mother—a refusal that is also a denial of his own sexuality. In coming to terms with this he will come to terms with life as a whole as this dichotomy is central. 'As his existence had two parents, so it had the earth and the sea. If his mother was the earth, his father was the sea.'[11] In *The Silver Darlings* it is Roddie and Catrine who represent these opposing tendencies—Roddie, swift and powerful like the sea, and Catrine calm and enduring like the earth. This dichotomy symbolises the two opposing inner drives which are tearing Finn—one towards security, the other towards exploring the unknown. And in this Finn's growth to maturity parallels his community's need to learn how to deal with the sea, terrifying and cruel, yet exhilarating and even kind. Maturity for Finn and for the community comes in learning how to balance these two apparently conflicting drives. This is a balance and integrity he recognises in Roddie, and in all that Finn does he is measuring himself against Roddie's standards.

But it is not only Finn who is aware of this quality in Roddie. He is held in high esteem by the men of Dunster. 'No man grudged Roddie his high distinction, because he was not only a daring and persevering seaman but also had the quiet independent mind that would curry favour with no one.' (p.78) At times this 'high distinction' becomes almost a supernatural awe, as at the end of Chapter 4. But it is his human qualities that make him so memorable. It is Roddie who guides Catrine on the last part of her journey to Caithness after the disappearance of Tormad. He is tall and fair, and the quietness and ease of his manner do much to comfort Catrine, newly arrived as a stranger, tired after her long journey. His considerate treatment of Catrine then links them in the reader's mind as a glimpse of what is to come.

Then and later Catrine is obviously attracted to Roddie, and is able to sense his feelings for her. Yet she holds back from involvement with him. On the surface, this is because there is still a possibility that Tormad might be alive, but Catrine knows within herself that he is dead. And her hanging back from Roddie stems from a determination to hold on to the security she has found in living in the house of Kirsty and her father. In a sense she uses that house as somewhere to hide from further involvement in the world, and after the birth of Finn she seems to live her life through him, denying her own nature. To enter into a relationship with Roddie would be to venture again into the unknown, and owing to the tragic circumstances surrounding her previous journey into this region, she is afraid to make herself so vulnerable again. It is no accident that Roddie is identified so strongly with the sea. Not only does Catrine hold herself back from the unknown in the shape of Roddie, but she also does her best to keep Finn away from the unknown which fascinates him—the sea. As a young child he tells his mother of his admiration for Roddie, and his love of the sea: ' "And when I'm big I'll go to sea, too, and be a skipper." "Mama does not want you to go to sea. You must never go to sea, Do you hear? Never." ' (p.144) Her vehemence stems from fear of the unknown which took her husband from her, and which now threatens to take her son. Finn is taken aback at this vehemence, but is not to be put off.

At the age of thirteen he has a narrow escape from the sea when he and another boy are trapped by the incoming tide while fishing from some rocks near the shore. The incident causes great tension between mother and son, and results in

Catrine trying to explain something of her hatred of the sea to Finn as they do their best to heal the rift between them.

> 'You mustn't be angry with me. The sea has not been kind to me. And then—we have been living here, though it is not our croft, our home . . . The only way we can pay back is if you —'
> She stopped, for though she knew what she was going to say was true enough . . . all were not so much reasons . . . as excuses for covering over the ultimate truth, which was simply her fear of what the sea might do to Finn; and because she knew this, and was honest in her ultimate self, she stopped talking . . .'
> (pp.173–4)

This admission is the beginning of Catrine's acknowledging that Finn is growing up, and that she can no longer hold him back. But in acknowledging Finn's separateness from her, she is also acknowledging her own individuality, which she has repressed for so long. This issues in a change of attitude towards Roddie, and leads to an incident which 'worked deeply' in Finn's mind.

At the celebration for the ending of the harvest, Finn, proud of his involvement in the man's world, misses Roddie in the house and goes out to speak to him in the byre. Just inside the byre door he comes upon Roddie and his mother. 'Catrine with her face white and scared and Roddie, a yard from her, silent. They looked at him but did not speak, and in that queer, still moment Finn's breast seemed to crush together and fall down inside him.' (p.176) This revelation is too much for Finn. He cannot take it in, and so tries to deny it:

> Roddie and his mother.
> He had never dreamt of anything between them. He knew all about flesh relations. He could not think . . .
> Roddie was thirty-eight and Catrine thirty-three. In Finn's thought they were fixed in their courses like the sun and the moon. They were old people.
> Suddenly he hated what he had seen, hated it in dumb frightened anger, hated its bodily crush, its tragic pallor, and moved swiftly on to the moor, as if the ghost of his father had come up behind him. (p.177)

74

The three central characters are here held in a suspension of awareness. Roddie and Catrine are apprehensive about Finn's reactions to their relationship, while for Finn himself, on the verge of manhood, restless and troubled by his own body this incident opens up before him a great chasm of uncertainty and confusion. Uncertain enough about his own identity, he sees that Roddie and Catrine, the two fixed poles in relation to which he is trying to define his own personality, are also capable of change. This whole complex of feelings is too much for Finn who rebels against it and shuts off his mind with anger and bitterness, turning away from Roddie and Catrine and more and more in on himself. 'After that night Finn cunningly hid things inside himself, yet at the same time found a greater release in life.' (p.177)

This release comes partly from his own sense of increasing individuality, and also from closing his mind to thoughts of Roddie and Catrine. But what he had recognised in their relationship is not to be denied and continues to gnaw at him from within, in his recognition of his own attraction to the girl Una. He had seen her first in the house of Meg the net-maker, and all the time Finn is growing up and learning his craft as a fisherman, he is deeply troubled by thoughts of Una. Always he is followed by a vision of her face, and by her eyes: 'Una did not laugh; her eyes lighted up and glanced. . . . They were wide-spaced, and in the dim light looked black. To Finn her clear face seemed so vivid, so unusual, that he wondered how others did not want to stare at her.' (p.184) He is troubled also by thoughts of her body. 'The dark body, with a red flame of life inside it, showing in the face, swaying with the grace of a tongue of fire.' (p.419) But these thoughts, whether from lack of physical experience or other cause, are never turgid and Finn's vision of Una draws him on, giving him increasing confidence to face the unknown.

This ability, however, is not achieved easily, but only through perseverance and patient endurance in times of threat. The coming of the plague to Dunster is another unknown which forces Finn to respond on a level beyond the personal. His mother's illness and Roddie's care and consideration for

Catrine, and for Finn himself, helps Finn to deal with the situation. On the surface the sexual tensions appear to fade into the background as the characters face the greater, impersonal power of death. Yet it is paradoxically at this very time when the three are drawn closer together that these tensions begin to become more intense. Finn is separated from his mother—she has sent him away for his own safety—and he is living in Roddie's house. Here, Roddie seems to fall naturally into the role of father to Finn, and through this contact with Roddie, Finn learns greater self-assurance and restraint. It is Roddie who prevents Finn from rushing in to his mother when she is weakened by illness:

> 'Listen, Finn. If you went in, what would your mother say? Damn it, boy, listen to me. Have sense. Do you want to go in and break her heart? . . . It's nothing for you or me to go in. That's easy. But what would your mother say? If she has the plague, God damn it, man, would it make her end easy to think she had given it to you, her son?' (p.267)

Thus it is from Roddie that Finn learns that man cannot control everything, that often he must bear the burden of failure by recognising the inevitable and not fighting against it. This is a lesson of responsibility and is one learned by Catrine at this same time, when the dying Kirsty makes her face up to reality:

> 'You'll never keep that boy from the sea. If you wish him well, don't try.'
> 'I do not want him to go to sea.'
> 'More ugly deaths on this land now than ever on sea. If you put that boy against his nature, you'll warp him. Remember that.' (p.239)

This, coupled with Finn's bravery and good sense during the time of plague, gives Catrine the confidence to let Finn go to sea with Roddie when it is all over. And it is Finn's going to sea that begins to break the impasse which has blocked the spontaneous growth of their various relationships.

Being at sea is a totally new experience for Finn, an experience which gives him a different perspective on things. Here he is part of the crew—sharing the discomfort, enjoying the jokes, simply 'belonging' in this group of men engaged in a common task. 'His old shy self had opened,' and with this opening up of his personality the whole complexion of life is changed. 'They all came alive, yet did not speak very much, for now started the exciting quest, that often grows tense, of finding an anchorage in an unknown place where shoal or submerged rock may at any moment hold the keel to disaster.' (p.287) The quest is the exploration of the unknown. Naturalistically this is the sea, with all its hidden dangers, and its exhilarations. But it is also an exploration of Finn's own mind in its response to this unknown.

A crucial moment in this process comes when Finn decides to climb the cliff-face in search of food and water for the rest of the crew. They have just survived a terrific storm and tempers are understandably frayed, yet Finn's decision goes beyond this. It is a direct challenge to Roddie, youth rebelling against maturity and good sense. This much is recognised by the others. But it is also something more:

> In their exhausted, thirst-tormented, overwrought condition, a bout of irritation or short temper was understandable enough, but the others felt that what had flared so swiftly between Roddie and Finn was deeper than irritation. They were like two with a blood-secret between them. (p.310)

In the end Roddie gives in to Finn's insistence, and takes the boat in so that Finn can begin his climb—a climb that once again is symbolic of Finn's striving for maturity. Yet his audacity is linked with his selfish desire to prove himself to the crew and also to slight Roddie. It is the 'triumph of enmity' that spurs him on. And, as earlier, he evades the reality of the situation by taking refuge in selfish anger and bitterness. For Roddie, fully conscious of the tangle linking him with Finn and Catrine, the climb is as great a test of endurance as it is for Finn. As Finn completes his climb Roddie is visibly relieved: 'Roddie, unknown to himself, groaned and sagged, completely exhausted. He had plumbed depths of fear and terror that Finn knew nothing of.' (p.316)

The confrontation between Roddie and Finn comes to a head after they have safely landed in Stornoway. Roddie is taunted by a local fisherman in a public house and a fight ensues. Finn moves towards Roddie in an effort to restrain him and encounters the man's explosive power. 'Roddie's left arm was still outstretched, the back of the open hand towards Finn's face. Through the foot that separated it from that face, Roddie brought it with such explosive force, that the resounding slap almost lifted Finn off his feet.' (p.360) This incident brings Finn face to face with Roddie's essential otherness, an otherness that he cannot penetrate, and which is capable of extreme violence if approached wrongly.

> More and more he realised that the eagerness and vanities that had beset him belonged to a youth which manhood, thickening its texture, kept in their place. He became one of the crew, seeing Roddie as an objective body and presence with which it was no business of his to interfere. Roddie wanted no more trouble. Neither did he. (pp.395–6)

In recognising this quality in Roddie he begins to see how it is also there in himself, and this leads to a renewed sense of freedom. And it is in this frame of mind that he returns home to Catrine. He is more assured, more distant, yet more considerate and feels his love for his mother more strongly as a bond between two separate individuals. He is also acutely aware of the presence of his father in that relationship: 'as they walked back to the house a deep feeling came over him of being himself and his own father, responsible for this woman walking by his side, who was his mother . . .' (p.411)

But the peace that comes from this increased sense of individuality is not enough. More and more Finn is drawn to the sea, which he sees as the masculine element, and his ambition is to have his own boat in order to hunt the herring. But it becomes clear to the reader that this involvement with the sea is partly a way of evading other aspects of life. Catrine, on the other hand, on receiving definite news of the death of her husband all those years before, is beginning to move towards a spiritual maturity corresponding to her physical maturity:

> She felt the rich flow of life in her flesh. Lately her body had had this deep warm feeling of well-being very strongly. Her skin had

the fairness that holds light. Her hair was fair. In the peat fire, her brown eyes looked black and gleamed with lights. (p.477)

Behind thought was feeling, charged with deeper meaning than thought. And this meaning was alive and immanent. (p.465)

Confirmation of Tormad's death, coupled with her own insight, frees Catrine to respond more fully to the present, and in particular to Roddie whose love she is now prepared to accept.

When Finn once again comes upon Roddie and his mother he too is pushed towards this 'deeper meaning than thought'. 'Everything stopped on the edge of thought, of apprehension. For he could not penetrate beyond the vision of Roddie and his mother.' (p.485) Finn is shaken to the core and is beset by guilt and horror. The thing is too close to him, too much a part of his own identity. Despite the maturity gained from his voyage to the West, and despite the increasing assurance of his manhood, he is unable and unwilling to probe too deeply in his mind. His initial confusion gradually gives way to a 'cold distaste' for both Roddie and Catrine, and it comes as a great relief to him when they are married and he is able to shut them out of his mind.

Once married, Roddie seems less and less drawn to the sea, while Finn goes more to it, in the spirit of testing himself against it. He has taken on Roddie's toughness but lacks his gentle calmness:

The weather was often wet and stormy, and occasionally it was intensely, bitterly cold. For spells, feeling would desert his hands and even the flesh on his back, and the cold would crawl along his bones . . . Not only his hands but his mind seemed washed by the cold sea water. (p.505)

This is Finn as the penitent, trying to cleanse himself of his impurities through the harshness of his work. Yet even here there is self-deception, and it becomes clear that Finn is using the sea as an avenue of escape. On the sea he might be strong and capable but he is also evading human responsibilities, to himself and others. At this stage of his life, he is not an attractive character.

But out of this pretence, the real Finn emerges, and does so in an incident that involves his acting selflessly on behalf of the community, and which brings Finn and Roddie closer. When a boat founders at the foot of the cliffs during a storm the people's mood of helplessness is broken when Finn decides to go down the cliff-face on a rope and attempt a rescue that way. And in an image that contrasts vividly with their previous encounter with a cliff-face, Roddie controls the rope from the top, the two men bringing together their outstanding and contrasting qualities— the audacity of youth and the calmness of experience. Their recognition of this is a moving acknowledgment of their separate strengths and weaknesses, and an acknowledgment of their need for each other:

> 'Are you ready?' asked Finn, and he met Roddie's eyes.
> 'Will you try it, boy?' asked Roddie, and his voice was gentle.
> It was á moment of communion so profound that Finn felt a light-heartedness and exaltation come upon him. This was where Roddie and himself met, in the region of comradeship that lies beyond all the trials of the world (p.513)

Although Finn and Roddie manage to save two men, two others are lost. But their coming together in the attempt to save the lives of others has lifted them beyond their personal tensions and the pettiness of their strained relationship. For Finn this is intensified by his genuine purgation in the death-coldness of the sea. The effect of this is to liberate Finn from his false idea of self, as in the rescue attempt his own life is so much bound up with the lives of other members of the community.

This is a liberation that is deepened by a voyage Finn takes to the Hebrides shortly afterwards. It is a journey he had longed to make for some time. 'He was longing to get away, longing for the sea-inlets of the West . . . It was like a land that existed in a dream, though he never had the felicity to dream of it except with his eyes open.' (p.506) On his earlier voyage to the Hebrides Finn had found a people different from his own, had been 'taken out of himself' simply by being in this new and exciting place. On this trip he is to discover a deeper affinity with the islands and their people. Forced to put in to North Uist by a threatening sea, Finn encounters a culture that has remained stable for centuries, in marked contrast to his own land caught in the grip of rapid economic and social change.

Finn is drawn to this people, and is aware of a great affinity with them which is explored through his responses to their story-telling, their singing, and their dancing, which has the effect of 'opening up' some of the blocked areas of his personality: 'as he listened something in himself that had hitherto been dry, like dry soil, was moistened as by summer rain, and became charged with an understirring of life.' (p.538)

Not only does Finn find much of value in this culture, but is himself able to contribute something to it. This he does in his telling of the story of his earlier voyage, which draws such high praise from Finn-son-of-Angus whose own story-telling had such an effect on Finn. What Finn has found is that elusive quality of wisdom. The reader is reminded of the Finn MacCool of Celtic legend who had captured 'the salmon of wisdom', and who is linked through this exploit to all the adolescent heroes in Gunn's novels of initiation. Through the two Finns, the storytellers, the continuity of a way of life is passed on in the form of wisdom, and insight.

The significance of North Uist in the story of Finn's development is that there he comes into direct contact with a culture that is wholly integrated. And through experiencing this sense of wholeness, Finn is able to see his own personality more clearly, is able to appreciate the need to develop this wholeness within himself by becoming more fully responsive to all areas of his psyche. This sense of wholeness and integration had been destroyed in his own society by the Clearances, but the fact that Finn responds to it so spontaneously is evidence of Gunn's belief that the drive for integration is basic in man: 'it would seem that to feel whole is a primary need of the self and comes in importance before any consideration of death, immortality or God.'[12] In this recognition of man's need for wholeness, Finn's journey to North Uist is clearly linked with the significance of his visits to the ruins known as Chapelhill or the House of Peace, near his home in Dunster. Both of these places are linked in Finn's mind through dream-imagery. Events in both of these places seem to go beyond Finn's normal range of thought. In part this is a link with those parts of the

81

book which use a culture's legends and superstitions to lend verisimilitude to the author's portrayal of that culture. But beyond this it is clearly linked to Finn's exploration of his own unconscious.

In both of these places Finn is taken beyond his normal self, and is made aware of a deeper potential for life within him. It is this opening up to an awareness of his own unconscious which marks the development of wisdom in Finn. While hiding his real feelings, his very real confusions, over his relationship with Roddie and Catrine by self-protective anger, the contact with North Uist and with the House of Peace helps to give Finn the sense of a stable 'centre' from which he can explore the world freely. Centred in this way in the second self there is no threat to his identity and so life can become the experience of delight. Once again the meditative process becomes apparent, as Finn learns to make contact with the still 'source' of his being.

Now a few broken walls on a small hill, the House of Peace had once been a monastery, and is a place of spiritual significance. Finn had early been aware of this, and found himself drawn to the place, despite the common belief that it was haunted. Even before he was born, Catrine had passed it with Roddie and had been affected by its abiding calmness. And as a child engaged in the pursuit of a butterfly, traditional symbol of the soul or psyche, Finn had found himself alone and afraid in this strange place. 'For the first time his loneliness came upon him in a great fear. He was so little that he could not run away and stood exposed in the centre of all the light in the world.' (p.95)

Even as a child Finn is aware of the nature of this place, but in his exhaustion he falls asleep, only to wake up to the terror of the void. 'For one terrible moment he was lost in the abyss of Nowhere, in a nightmare of sunlight and strange appearances.' (p.95) But he has the strength of character to live through this moment of panic, and find the serenity beyond.

Over the years Finn had returned often to the House of Peace, and in all his changing moods it remains a place of quiet and stability, a place where he can easily feel the living reality of his second self.

It was always sheltered here and bright, as if the light itself slept or, rather, lay awake in the dreaming pleasantness that sometimes comes on the body when, bare-legged, it curls in the sun. Perhaps the brightness came, too, from the grey stone; brightness and silence. Finn's mind always quickened as he looked around, and hearing and sight became acute.

By all the superstitions, he should be frightened of this place. And he was—a little, as if a tiny pulse of panic might beat at any time. But he liked this feeling, too. It lay beyond the need to show courage, to have his mind emptied and his body taut, as though there was also a friendliness, and intimacy, withdrawn and evasive. (p.213)

In this frame of mind—relaxed yet alert—Finn is aware of the creative potential of the void; the initial panic is quietly controlled, and the emptiness is seen not as threatening but as liberating. And in this same state of mind Finn has a startling experience at the House of Peace. Unsure as to whether he is awake or dreaming he sees the figure of an old man in a white cape who simply stands and looks at him, an action that is eloquent beyond speech:

> . . . the look was extraordinarily full of understanding, and somewhere in it there was a faint humour, the humour that knows and appreciates and yet would not smile to hurt, yet the smile was there. It knew all about Finn, and told him nothing—not out of compassion, but out of needlessness. (p.214)

This strange encounter leaves Finn with 'a feeling of ease and comfort', and it is clear that the figure of the old man embodies those qualities which Finn lacks—understanding and tolerance—and is an image of the state of wisdom, an image which helps Finn on his growth to maturity. The encounter seals his awareness of the significance of the House of Peace in this process.

The wisdom of maturity that Finn is seeking is a wisdom that fully acknowledges all aspects of the personality. It is a wisdom that he recognises in the culture of North Uist. And contact with this culture gives him the courage to look openly at his relationship with Roddie and his mother. For Finn the meaning of this balanced culture is given focus in his own love for a girl of the island, a love which allows him a different perspective on his mother's love for Roddie, and for himself: 'He was fond of her, would ever have for her a natural affection, but he saw her now as a woman under the spell of her own destiny. And that somehow was eternally right . . . And this brought to him, beyond understanding, a cool aloof relief.' (p.549) There is no way Finn can grasp this truth on a conscious level. Through his encounter with the Lewis girl something in him has changed, and he is able to accept that his mother has her own life, which is lived apart from him. Once he can understand this it is no longer felt as a threat, and inner conflict gives way to acceptance. This is as it should be. It is the capacity Jung noticed in his patients to 'outgrow' a problem, the capacity not to solve it on the intellectual level, but to learn to live through it and so defuse its destructive potential. The problems, Jung noted,[13] were not solved logically, but 'faded out' when confronted with 'a new and stronger life-tendency'. This process he connects specifically with the 'unforced action' of *wu-wei*, in a passage which highlights the universality and spontaneity of the process of meditation.

> What then did these people do in order to achieve the progress that freed them? As far as I could see they did nothing (*wu-wei*), but let things happen . . . The art of letting things happen, action in non-action, letting go of oneself, as taught by Master Eckehart, became a key to me with which I was able to open the door to the 'Way'. The key is this: we must be able to let things happen in the psyche. For us, this becomes a real art of which few people know anything. Consciousness is forever interfering, helping, correcting, and negating, and never leaving the simple growth of the psychic processes in peace. It would be a simple enough thing to do, if only simplicity were not the most difficult of all things.[14]

For Finn in *The Silver Darlings*, the 'new and stronger life-tendency' is the awareness of his own sexuality, which for many years he had stubbornly held at bay, especially as regards his mother, but also concerning the girl Una. Yet even after his return from North Uist he tries to deny this, seeing the 'culminating act in his growth towards responsible manhood' as being the ownership of a new boat. But the natural way of things is not to be denied, as Finn discovers when he goes to the House of Peace to meditate on this new idea. At the House of Peace he cannot find the peace of mind he is seeking, and becomes tired and wretched. Peace of mind will not come until he penetrates all his self-deceptions and evasions to the core. This is the real rite of purgation, and in the centre of his being Finn must acknowledge Una, who had always been the only person able to penetrate the circle of his defences. In the end he has to acknowledge this, and in a full acceptance of the *wholeness* of his own individuality encompassing every facet of his personality, he is able to recognise his need for Una.

With Finn's going to Una, the novel could end. But Gunn has added a last symbolic chapter which makes use of the *mandala* image to suggest his achievement of wholeness and integration. The chapter is entitled 'Finn in the Heart of the Circle', and shows Finn on the eve of his marriage to Una, trying to evade his friends who are intent on putting him through 'certain heathenish practices' by way of initiation into this new stage of his life. He is determined to outwit them, and seeks refuge at the House of Peace. 'When he was assured that no one was after him, he performed the mental act of describing the circle of sanctuary round the ground on which he lay. Then his eyes fell on the circle of low flat stones and he crept into its heart.' (p.580) In the heart of this circle Finn is united with Una and the book ends with this image of Finn in the heart of this circle, with life coming for him. He is able to see himself as a white-haired old man sitting here many years from now. This is the old man of his earlier vision; an image of the wisdom to which he has now attained, a wisdom that does not try to halt the process of life and examine it piece by piece, but rather is completely responsive and alive to the living moment itself. This kind of awareness is not an end; it is only the beginning. 'What he had lived of life was only its beginning. Its deeper mysteries were ahead.' (p.583)

SLAYING THE MIND
The Serpent 1943

Like *The Silver Darlings, The Serpent* (1943) is also concerned with the attainment of wisdom, with the liberation of the individual from the 'blocks' which obscure his proper relation to 'The Way of Heaven', and lead to feelings of separation and alienation. With the attainment of wisdom and the insight of understanding comes the realisation that one is, at one and the same time, both a fully-developed individual *and* an integral part of a much larger, more comprehensive process. In exploring this theme *The Serpent* has obvious affinities with the *The Silver Darlings*, where the relation of the individual to a larger communal reality is examined through the relationship of Finn with Roddie and Catrine. But it is with the earlier *Highland River* that the book has a more specific connection. The central situation, the situation from which the novel's structure is derived, is identical to that of *Highland River*; the portrayal of the state of mind of a man meditating on past and present experience, engaged in the archetypal quest for that which is constant in the heart of change.

In *The Serpent*, the story of Tom Mathieson is told in flashbacks, as he climbs the hill above his village, stopping occasionally to regain his breath. Now an old man, he thinks back over the events of his life and is able to perceive their unity, a far cry from the chaos of those events at the time. The climb is a symbol of every man's journey through life, a journey punctuated by moments of inactivity and rest in which new insights are fully assimilated. At the end of the book Tom dies while resting near the top of the hill, and the circle of his life is closed. As Edwin Muir pointed out, it is from this life that the novel takes its unity, from the portrayal of the events of one man's life being recalled during the tiring journey towards a better vantage point. 'The unity of the story is the unity of one man's experience as seen by himself shortly before his death, when the pattern has already woven itself, and by turning round he can see it spread out before him.'[1]

Essentially this process of going over the events of one's life is the process of meditation and *The Serpent*, like *Highland River*, gives the reader an insight into the workings of that process. In *The Serpent* the quest may be the same, but it is less conscious than Kenn's quest for the source. The meditative process revealed as the old man reflects on his life is more specific than that explored in *Highland River* and shows clearly how Tom's inherent spontaneity had been blocked at certain times, and how there seemed no easy way out of those situations. This is in contrast to the 'lightness' which characterises Kenn's quest in the earlier novel. In this *The Serpent* is closer to the lengthy process of Enlightenment undergone by Finn in *The Silver Darlings*. But for Tom Mathieson in *The Serpent*, the attainment of Enlightenment has been a more harrowing experience because it is in the very nature of the quest that each man must find the answer for himself, in his own way. Despite its universal nature, the experience is intimate and personal. This is one of the central lessons of the novel:

> So he came back to the individual, and as the only individual he would ever have a chance of knowing was himself, he drifted from his preoccupations with socialism and freethought into a tentative reading of philosophy. For manifestly each individual was born by himself, lived by himself, and died by himself. There was no getting past that. That was central. All the rest that was added to it, was superstructure. (p.234)

The story is told from Tom's point of view, from his hard-won state of detachment and awareness. Taken in its entirety, the novel traces the process by which Tom is able to cast off the habits of conceptual or conditioned thought,[2] and it shows clearly how Enlightenment comes not from adding on new ideas, new intellectual accomplishments, but rather from the stripping away of false ideas *about* reality in order to perceive that reality as it is. His journey has given him the strength and the ability to live with what Watts has called 'the wisdom of insecurity', the ability to forget about 'self', and to engage directly with the reality of a situation so that action is spontaneous and 'right', because it is in harmony with Tao.[3]

The reader's involvement with Tom's thought-processes starts with the opening sentence of the book, where he is placed *inside* the main character: 'As the Philosopher paused on the upward slope to let out a stream of breath he felt the beating of his heart and heard its dark buzz in his ears.' (p.5) From this moment on the reader sees what this other sees and is made gradually aware of the past details of Tom's life. But more immediately he is made aware of the world as Tom sees it now; the world seen through the eyes of wisdom, the landscape of delight:

> . . . this deliberate seeing of his past had a certain detached interest, giving to the flight of a chaffinch, to its short airy waves of flight, an indescribable pleasure. How clean and bright were the feathers this sunny day, how vivid and immediate the song and the movement! The dip of the branch, the swaying of the green leaf. The green grass and the warm scents and the wind that found its pleasure not in far wandering but in immediate eddies of fun among the small bushes. (p.32)

This image does not simply give an objective description of Tom's surroundings. Rather it is meant to convey to the reader something of his detached but joyful state of mind. The image is not all of the truth, but it focuses man's mind in a way that allows him to perceive it. This is an important idea in *The Serpent*, and indeed in Gunn as a whole, that things too deep for thought can best be expressed through images. 'The Philosopher smiled lightly to himself as he always did when an image entered and crystallised a mood of thought or reverie. This was one of life's rarer possessions or capacities. And when the image formed and passed the mind was freed and uplifted.' (p.114) Thus this vision of life as delight is no evasion of Tom's past, but is rather a 'crystallisation' and fulfilment of it. It is precisely because of his intimate personal knowledge of the darker side of life that he is able to respond so freely to the vision of the world as indeed 'delight-full'. In this main structural device of the novel past memory and present awareness are skilfully counterpointed as Gunn builds up a fully-rounded character. Every so often the reader's attention is drawn to the *now* of the novel which is Tom's slow ascent of the hill, and his detached tone of voice which is the voice of a man who has been through it all and has something important to say, something which cannot be formulated intellectually but which must be grasped directly.

Tom is able to laugh at his youthful folly and at his later exaggerated seriousness. But there is never any evasion of the real pain and distress which he had caused by those very qualities which he recognises now as a young man's absurdities. It is this quiet tone of voice that engages the reader's sympathies from the beginning for a character who in many ways might seem undeserving of that sympathy. And it is this voice, the commenting voice of the older and wiser man, which guides the reader through the traumatic events of his story. It is the quiet tone of voice of a man who is able to see clearly the delight which underlies all human experience. This voice, calmly examining the unity of one man's life, crystallises for the reader the quality of detachment, and gives him an insight into the mind of wisdom.

> He who is wise sees near and far
> As the same,
> Does not despise the small
> Or value the great:
> Where all standards differ
> How can you compare?
> With one glance
> He takes in past and present,
> Without sorrow for the past
> Or impatience with the present.
> All is in movement.
> He has experience

Of fullness and emptiness.
He does not rejoice in success
Or lament in failure
The game is never over
Birth and death are even
The terms are not final.[4]

But this capacity for detachment is hard won. Tom's story is a grim, at times melodramatic story of one man's struggle towards Enlightenment and an account of the suffering which that struggle causes both in himself and to those around him. For long stretches of the book it is clear that he is under a great deal of strain while it is left to the reader to decide for himself how far he can accept Tom's testimony; whether he is in fact wholly sane at certain crucial points in the narrative. All of this is part of the complexity of Gunn's portrayal of 'modern' man, the sceptic.

As befits a story of intense personal upheaval, *The Serpent* is set during a period of rapid social and psychological change. Gunn himself drew attention to this aspect of the book in a letter to Iain MacArthur of Club Leabhar who republished *The Serpent* in 1970:

> It covers a remarkable time of transition in Highland history, as I may have said before, from the old hand-threshing machine, the hard-tyred bike, to the motor car and smart country garage, on the economic side; and on the religious from the old rigid puritanism to the tentative and often highly dramatic introduction of agnosticism and freethought . . .[5]

The same point is made in Chapter 14 of the novel where Tom talks over old times with the shepherd on the hill. And near the end of his climb he sees his own period as:

> A period of social and economic change, a 'transition era' from the old self-sufficiency of the croft in work and thought and Gaelic culture to – this world of today, itself vastly unstable and heading perhaps for future wars on a gigantic scale.
>
> All that as the background – or foreground – affecting individual action and reaction. For he must never forget again that what was important in social change was the effect on the individual. (p.233)

91

Again we come back to the personal nature of the quest, an idea of great importance to Gunn as we can see not only from the novels, but also from diary entries and from magazine and newspaper articles:

> Behind all the calculations of the intellect, behind the megalomania of a leader, behind the religion of an economic system, there is that individual, the individual who suffers, who dies, who loves. When we forget that individual, when we forget to pay tribute, above all things, to the living core and flame of the individual life, at that moment we are heading for the organisation of death.[6]

The subjugation of the individual to the mass is what he saw as 'the great modern heresy':

> It is an implicit denial of the freedom of the adventuring individual spirit; ideally it is an effort, in time of great difficulty and danger, amid a destructive welter of conflicting ideas, to round man up and drive him back into a state of stable security, such as the security of the beehive, with its perfect economic efficiency and corporate consciousness.[7]

Among the novels perhaps the most explicit treatment of this theme is to be found in *The Green Isle of the Great Deep*. But *The Serpent* also traces clearly the growth of this realisation in the mind of a man who had, in his time, been part of various orthodoxies, including the orthodoxies of freethought and scepticism:

> You have got to watch them or they'll get you, each one of them: atheist, socialist, psychologist, philosopher, religious. Each is ready to take you 'the only way'.
> How could there be so many philosophies, so many 'perfect systems', each contradicting the other on the vital issues, if each were not a manifestation of a purely personal bias or need, an emotional fulfilment, of the individual philosopher?
> That's what it came down to in the end. (p.67)

In the end 'the only way' is a deeper scepticism, one which eschews all concepts and sees reality directly. The world seen in terms of intellectual concepts and formulae might appear simple and easy to put to rights but the complexity of the reality is always too great.

Do you think you can take over the universe and improve it?
I do not believe it can be done.

The universe is sacred.
You cannot improve it.
If you try to change it, you will ruin it.
If you try to hold it, you will lose it.[8]

What is required, as Eastern thinkers have long recognised, is a more comprehensive vision which takes into account the larger movements of this 'sacred' universe in which man has his being. This is stated unequivocally by Krishnamurti: 'revolution in society must begin with the inner, psychological transformation of the individual.'[9] And it is so because 'the world is not separate from us; we are the world, and our problems are the world's problems'.[10] Taoism also understood this important insight which it expressed in the vision of an ordered cosmos:

Man follows the earth.
Earth follows heaven.
Heaven follows Tao.
Tao follows what is natural.[11]

In *The Serpent* Tom's gradual understanding of this is clearly marked by the various structural divisions of the book which take him from the Highlands to the city, and back again to the Highlands. The physical shifts of the novel mirror Tom's shifting attempts to gain self-knowledge. At each of these stages of his life we see him seeking some kind of meaning or significance in existence.

The quest begins in Glasgow where, after becoming acclimatised to his new environment Tom is drawn into the intellectual ferment of the city. This is largely due to the influence of Dougal Robertson, his boss. It is Dougal who tells him of the 'Idols of the Tribe', who highlights for him the power of the Church, and who reveals something of the way in which man's thinking is conditioned by social institutions. At first Tom is aware only of his own ignorance, particularly when Dougal asks him about his own area, but gradually he gains the confidence to think out some of these things for himself:

> That was the beginning of the awakening of his mind. The books
> he borrowed from Dougal were brighter and more exciting than
> any chance toy or 'bonnie thing' he had ever got as a child. Their
> arguments were so clear, so obviously incontrovertible, that they
> had about them the quality of laughter. (p.15)

The Glasgow period is a time of excitement, a time of
expansion, in which Tom first glimpses something of human
potential. Yet even while undergoing this 'awakening of the
mind' there is a darker side to his Glasgow experiences.

In encountering this new world of intellectual fervour Tom is
forced to reconsider many of his basic assumptions, assumptions
which are identical with those of many people whom he had re-
spected in his native community. This leads inevitably to a degree
of uncertainty as to just who is right, and to what extent his
new ideas cut off much of what he had accepted before. The
experience causes a disturbing 'division' in Tom's mind to which
he reacts by becoming too certain, too sure of himself, and
unnecessarily brutal in argument, finding a perverse delight in
the exercise of logic, 'the instrument of the freethinker that was
more precise and exquisite in its work than any turning lathe.'
(p.16) Later, he openly acknowledges this split in himself.

> To tell the truth, much of what he had read in criticism of the Bible
> had secretly repelled him. He saw the force of what was written,
> but was repelled by the spirit of the writer, by what appeared a
> sheer destructiveness for its own sake. At least, it had often made
> him uncomfortable. (p.143)

And throughout the book Tom is seen assessing and evaluating
his personality at various stages of his development. It is
perhaps this trait above all which engages the reader's sympathy. This candid revelation of uncertainty is important in the
description of a character who is seen to move through the
novel from a position of rebellion and bitterness, to a state of
acceptance and humility. By showing that even in the heart of
rebellion there is uncertainty and doubt Gunn is able to show
that rebellion and acceptance are not at all the irreconcilable
opposites they at first appear, but are parts of one process, the
growth of wisdom and understanding.

The Glasgow phase ended prematurely by his father's illness, Tom returns to the Highlands where his new ideas inevitably clash with many of the traditional values of the community. At first, however, the change is welcome. His assumption of the role of provider for the house brings with it a new sense of responsibility and importance. 'It had been exceptionally good harvest weather and on the whole he had enjoyed the work. After the first week, when his body had got all muscle-bound, he experienced, for the first time in his life consciously, a rare sense of physical well-being.' (p.34) This 'rare sense of physical well-being', arising from contact with the land, foreshadows the later 'liberation of the hills' which sustains him through the most crucial period of his life.

But this feeling does not last and a great deal of strain and tension becomes apparent in the relationship between Tom and his father, once strong and capable but now almost totally dependent on others. The process of estrangement is gradual but irrevocable and Gunn traces it masterfully, clearly involving the reader's sympathies with both men, and with the mother who is caught helpless between them.

The conflict between the two men gradually becomes focussed around two central issues—Tom's atheism, and his desire to start up a small business. And here it becomes apparent that the conflict is essentially the age-old battle between the traditional and the modern. Adam Mathieson, with his Old Testament theology and his dislike of Tom's attempts to better himself by starting a business, represents the old ways which are being worn away by the enthusiasm and vigour of the modern, which here finds its expression in Tom's questioning of the spiritual authority of the Bible, and his attempt to change, even in a small way, a social structure he sees as brutally restrictive. The two men are separated by a lack of understanding of the nature of change. As Tom's mother explains, the older man sees no need for change, indeed fears it as it seems to undermine the very foundations of his sense of self: ' "If the croft and the carting kept us and a decent house over our heads he thinks it should be good enough for you. Then he got on again about— about the other thing".' (p.78) This short speech links Tom's social ideas with his religious standpoint and highlights the central motive force of the book—the need to understand the process of change, which is the process of life itself.

At this same time Tom's life has entered a new phase, through his involvement with Janet, a relationship that gives him a renewed confidence, a new sense of self. The growth of their love is traced by Gunn with honesty and delicacy, and it is clear that in this relationship Tom finds something to counterbalance the bitterness and frustration which has come to characterise his home life. But it is something intangible, something not to be explained away in the terms of logic. The suddenness, the irrationality of this, is highlighted by its happening to him, the Philosopher, the man of logic: 'his intellectual assurance had been dealt one of those invisible blows that scatter elements in a bewildering fashion.' (p.57)

The relationship with Janet is also the beginning of an awakening to the land which is to prove a sustaining force in his life:

> It was then no doubt, imperceptibly, little by little, that there was born in him a first real intimacy with the earth, the earth of his own land.
> Imperceptibly, because at first it was not the earth but Janet. The earth was merely his fellow conspirator. He could call it to witness silently, when he came into the hollow where Janet and himself had met in the dark. (pp.72–3)

This vision is able to sustain him because, through it, he is able to see that there is an order in change, that change itself is a constant in human experience. 'A land that changed from bend to corner, from ridge to crest, yet had that in it from ancient time that did not change.' (p.113) For Tom, his love for Janet is a positive step in his quest for wisdom. From Janet he learns something more important than he had learned in Glasgow. For in Glasgow his awakening had been mainly intellectual. With Janet he has gone beyond this, beyond abstraction, to direct contact with the intensity of life. The link between Janet and the earth is crucial, as it is the beginning of an awareness in Tom of how his own community is more complex than his intellectual analysis had recognised. From this time on he is prepared to see that there is much of value in the traditions of that community.

At the time, however, it is but a glimmer of awareness, and just as the religious conflict with his father is drawing nearer a crisis point, he begins to sense a change in Janet's feelings for him. Since taking up a job at the manse she had seemed more distant, and it is only a matter of time before Tom realises that she is now more attracted to Donald than to himself. Both matters come to a head in Chapter 12, when he is very bitter about Janet's betrayal of his love:

> The hours, the days, that followed had a bitterness, an inner cruelty that changed his nature, hardened and shaped it blade-sharp.
> And the blade was turned on himself. Inwardly it cut and twisted, shearing off the soft adhesions of sentiment, of tender belief, whose existence he now regarded with an excruciating mockery. (p.140)

It is while he is in this frame of mind that he is confronted by William Bulbreac, a Kirk elder and one of the community's narrower and nastier minds. Cunningly Bulbreac draws Tom into a furious argument in the course of which he brands him with the mark of the serpent: 'For I see the serpent within you, I see its evil coils twisting in your body and in your brain, and I see that you have delivered yourself to the serpent . . .' (p.131) At the height of this argument, Tom's father enters and attempts to strike him, to kill the serpent of evil.

> The grey face, the grey beard, the blazing eyes, the silent pursuing face—it had come at last. The power of the father created in the image of God. The tribal power, the unearthly power. Each felt it, and Tom could not move.
> The father gazed upon his son with a fixity of expression more terrible than all words. In silence he groped for William's staff. He took a slow step nearer to his son, and, in the short pause that followed, the intention of chastisement gathered in a concentration horrible to behold. Then the hand with the staff went up, not quickly, but with deliberation. It rose, until it rose high above his head, then all in a moment the stiffness of the arm slackened, the stick fell, bouncing off Tom's chest, the arm wavered down, the body sagged, and with a deep grunt it collapsed upon itself, pitching forwards slightly before Tom's feet. (pp.151–2)

The Old Testament overtones are clear. The evil of the serpent has prevailed, and from this time on Tom is known as the atheist who killed his own father.

Tom's despair following the death of his father is intensified by the strain put on him by the community's response to that death. His shop windows are smashed and the ideas he is taken to represent are bitterly denounced by the minister in a sermon which encourages the people to regard the world dualistically, as a war of Good against Evil, and so to take sides against Tom, the Evil One.

Rejected by the people he has lived among all his life, Tom is thrown back more and more on himself, driven to an unceasing examination of all the values involved in his situation. For him there are no easy answers. The knowledge gained in Glasgow is no longer enough. And the 'appalling stress' of this situation, does 'extreme violence' to his nature, leading to physical and mental exhaustion, and to a dumb heedlessness of the life going on around him. His general anxiety becomes focussed in the hallucinatory vision of a strange beast. The beast is horrific enough in itself, but the real horror is that its face is always hidden, always turned away. 'In moments of extreme horror and disintegration', Tom is haunted by the fear that the beast will turn its face and look at him, a fear closely linked to the death of his father whose face has also pursued him. The climax of his illness comes when he sees his dead father standing by the corner of the stubblefield, watching him. This vision leads directly to his inevitable collapse.

Yet this collapse is not total. There is still a central 'core' to Tom's personality, an 'ultimate centre' and 'continuing essence' that is able to endure this assault: 'through all these experiences there remained the final core that was himself, something beyond his moods and visions, beyond his nature even. It was a small core, sometimes little more than a cry, but it remained.' (p.168) This core is of course the 'second self'. In *The Serpent* it is clearly linked with the land, with the earth itself, as evidenced in Tom's love-affair with Janet. This second self recognises its affinity with that which is unchanging in this landscape. And it is through his failures, through the intensity of suffering, that

Tom is brought into healing contact with this deeper aspect of himself.

Under his mother's care, he gradually recovers from his fever, and it seems that he has now won a new peace, but it is soon clear that this sense of peace is also illusory. His home is now 'like a burrow, a secure bolt-hole from the outside world', and Tom himself seems unconsciously aware of the fact that he is trying to evade something. 'Sometimes, as his eyes cast about to make sure there was no-one near, he experienced the criminal feeling of one in hiding.' (p.192) As always the evasion is ultimately the evasion of self-knowledge and awareness. Tom burrows into his illusory ego, to evade the reality of his second self. And it is only when he is prepared to acknowledge the less conscious aspects of his personality that he is able to glimpse the reality of freedom. This process of opening up to all aspects of himself is symbolised by his journey to the Lowlands, and his resolution to murder Donald, a journey which makes him fully aware of the darker side of his personality. After this the horrific circumstances of Janet's death make him aware that this darkness is not only in him, but is part of life's total pattern.

This ability to see life as a process is the beginning of wisdom, for it frees man from his sense of alienation from his environment, by making him aware that change is not violent and arbitrary but is part of an organic order.

> The concept of change is not an external, normative principle that imprints itself upon phenomena; it is an inner tendency according to which development takes place naturally and spontaneously. Development is not a fate dictated from without to which one must silently submit, but rather a sign showing the direction that decisions take. Again, development is not a moral law that one is constrained to obey; it is rather the guideline from which one can read off events. To stand in the stream of this development is a datum of nature; to recognise it and follow it is responsibility and free choice.[12]

Change is in the nature of things; 'reversal is the movement of Tao'. When something reaches its extreme, it changes into its opposite, so that life is a continual process of interaction of *yin*

99

and *yang*. The wise man is one who understands this process and is able to hold the two in a dynamic balance.

For Tom, for Gunn himself, the traditions of his own community are vital to the realisation of this. It was against the traditional framework of his society that Tom had initially rebelled, only to discover that, try as he might to cast off its influence, it is impossible: the very nature of his rebellion is conditioned by that society. It is this insight which frees him, enabling him to see the traditions of his people not as a set of rules attempting to contain life, but rather as a creative response to the business of living in its entirety. And when he explains his 'natural anarchy' to the shepherd on the hill, he attributes it not to his Glasgow experiences, but to his early upbringing in this very place:

> '. . . you had the individual responsible for his own bit of land, while at the same time he was an active member of the community, abiding by its customs and laws, just as his own bit of land was part of the communal land . . . a true balance between the maximum freedom of the individual and the common welfare of all, and at the same time—and this is where the anarchism comes in—they had no bosses, no tyrants, no bureaucrats, no profit-drivers among themselves . . .' (pp.176–7)

In *The Serpent* the idea of tradition as a creative response to living is represented by Tom's mother, and to a lesser extent by Janet. Always, however, it is tied to the earth and to the female. George Bruce has commented on the way in which Tom's mother is described, like Dark Mairi, in earth imagery at a crucial moment in the plot.[13] And as Tom himself tells the shepherd, the earth is central to his understanding of life: 'She is pretty nearly my philosophy, my religion, and everything now. But she has taken a lot of knowing.' (p.178)

But life also, as Tom is forced to acknowledge, has its destructive side. Janet's death is a last devastating blow to his assurance, and the ending of the novel describes his coming to terms with this.

Janet's death brought about in Tom an 'extreme despondency' so severe that he had run away in an effort to escape from it: 'a remarkable odyssey, containing some weird and memorable scenes. It lasted barely five weeks, yet . . . it had the air of a journey to another world.' (p.231) It had been a journey into 'vast unpeopled spaces', a journey into the void of himself and so a microcosm of the whole book. In this encounter with the void, Tom is made fully aware of the illusory nature of his ego, and through a full acceptance of this, and in accordance with the laws of change, his attitude undergoes a reversal, a 'turning about in the deepest seat of consciousness' as the Lankāvatāra Sūtra puts it:

> And then in the midst of that desolation, with the fine rain smothering the view like a clinging smoke, wet and cold and miserable, he had felt so far beyond all mortal care, so stripped of the last vestige of desire, so finally and wholly the outcast, that a rare thin delight, like a wintry sunlight, had for a time lit up his soul and glimmered in his sight. (pp.231–2)

This recognition of delight in the heart of desolation is the insight which gives Tom the strength to endure. He stops running, and returns home.

The return home is a returning to the source, to a renewal of the link between each individual and life's creative energy. In Tom's case this is a return to the traditional values of the community, not as an empty assumption of traditional roles but at a much deeper level. This is not a denial of his earlier criticisms of that society, but is an attitude based on the realisation that true wisdom will never be attained through the power of the rational mind divorced from the human virtue of compassion.

This lesson he had learned from his community, and in particular from the way in which the values of that community were embodied in his mother so it is fitting that the debt is acknowledged in the tenderness with which Tom nurses his mother through her last illness. This is of course a physical tenderness, but more importantly it is the tact and delicacy with which he is able at last to explain to her something of those earlier attitudes by which he had caused so much pain and suffering. He tells her of his interest in David Hume, he talks of his questioning of the spiritual authority of the Church, but most important of all he demonstrates his changed attitude by offering to read the Bible to her. This reading is a great comfort to her, and to Tom it is in the nature of a revelation. Able now to regard the book objectively he is able to appreciate its portrayal of life in its wholeness:

> Nothing was suppressed. Goodness was here but so was vice. Songs of praise and gladness, the tribulations of utter misery. And gathered in clusters, amid the buzzing and stinging and slaughter, were the cells that held the golden honey of wisdom.
> No wonder such a human record had kept its hold on a living humanity. (p.242)

And it is revealing that when he does try to account for his earlier scepticism, his accusations are directed not at the figure of Christ, but rather at those who corrupt His message in the interest of personal power and gain.

This more compassionate outlook had also been engendered by certain connections Tom had made between his reading and his personal experience. At this level, philosophy is no longer theory; it takes on its own intense reality. In reading some of the letters which had passed between Hume and Rousseau, he becomes aware of an essential difference between the two men, a difference which he now sees had been of great significance in his own life:

> Just as Hume's essential attitude to life, on which his principles were based, was different from Rousseau's, so was the male attitude from the feminine. He began to perceive definitions of justice, beauty, chastity, truth, not as absolutes but as masculine conceptions. . . . (p.238)

In the realisation of the dichotomy between the male world of concepts and abstractions and the female world of intuition, he recognises himself and Janet, and his mother:

> . . . he saw now how vivid a woman's apprehension of the real was. A man could cloud his apprehension with all sorts of rules, categories, principles, theories. Not so a woman. She saw what she wanted, the inner kernel, the thing-in-itself, and went, by some law of her feminine being, unerringly for that. (p.240)

This is the lesson Tom has learned; intellect alone will never solve the world's problems. Something else is required, something which reaches out beyond the known and helps man expand into freedom.

> Love. Well, there was love. Just as there was suffering. Suffering by itself brutalised. But suffering transformed by love—than that man knows nothing more profound. Just nothing. It was the ultimate experience, the ultimate cleansing . . . short of death, that enigma. (p.252)

Love, unlike the intellect, cannot be forced. It must happen spontaneously, and can only emerge when one is open and receptive; through the adoption of what, to the male mind, seem female attitudes. By the adoption of a more yielding and flexible attitude to experience one learns how to control circumstances by going along with their natural movement. This is the 'virtue of non-contention' which is one of the central lessons of the *Tao Te Ching*.

> This is called the perception of the nature of things.
> Soft and weak overcome hard and strong.[14]

> Yielding to force is strength.[15]

Something of Tom's understanding of this principle is conveyed to the reader by the way in which the ending of the novel once again draws attention to the reality of the old man slowly climbing the hill. The quietness and inevitability of his death at the end of that climb is a fitting end to the novel, emphasising as it does the futility of 'thought' when faced with the mystery of existence. It is fitting also that death takes place on the open hillside which has meant so much to Tom throughout the book. Contact with the land had given him glimpses of freedom, as the ego and its problems has no hold in this region. Such contact had always been 'enlivening' and 'invigorating', and had given him renewed strength and vitality. To understand and consciously seek such renewal from the 'source', is the process of meditation, the finding of the second self. Initially the realisation is daunting as it reveals to man the emptiness of his habitual sense of self. But gradually this feeling of emptiness is felt as liberating and allows man to expand into freedom. Recognition of the essential emptiness of self and world is a necessary precondition for awakening as it is a withdrawal from involvement with the illusory world of *māyā*, and its gaiety, its delight comes from this sense of liberation. Looking around him at the world, Tom is able to sense this.

> The Philosopher was no methodical naturalist; indeed he felt himself like nothing very much at all. And in this nothing much there was a freedom, an acceptance, a participation, a part of everything-in-itself, that had a humour subtly produced as honey. (p.251)

This sense of being 'nothing very much at all' is like the Buddha's claim that he gained nothing from unexcelled complete enlightenment, for which very reason it is called unexcelled complete enlightenment. It is a quiet awareness of reality which transcends the personal without destroying it. It is the beginning of true meditation. And Gunn in a very short space takes the reader from the world of conceptual thinking, deep into the heart of the experience of meditation.

> The Philosopher settled himself comfortably and his heart expanded in tribute. Indeed for a little while his eyes closed under the snout of his bonnet and he floated deep and away. Not wishing, however, to lose altogether this solitary delight, this pagan sensation, he half-opened his eyes, so that he only half-slept, a temporary in-between state which permitted what was heavy to dissolve quite away . . .
>
> Presently not only his mind but his eyes and his ears and the skin inside his clothes came delicately alive . . . He smiled in divine ease, for if all he heard was the song in his own blood, that blood came out of ocean and earth and sky and would return thither. Not much separated one element from another. Not much—but yet how exquisite the little, the little that separated being from not-being . . .
>
> His chin fell to his chest, his eyes to the heather by his upturned toes, for in this attitude sight went more readily inward, identifying itself with those inner eyes that produced the light by which thought was made visible.
>
> He knew the moment of extreme pause when it seems that the veil which divides being from not-being becomes filmy, verges on complete translucence. Here the last illusion seems to be dispelled and time in stillness completes itself; the beginning and the end are comprehended. (pp.253–4)

THE WORLD OF LIGHT
The Well at the World's End 1951

The Serpent shows how thought in the end exhausts itself and gives way to a more creative and flexible response to experience. *The Well at the World's End* (1951) is an attempt to evoke the reality of that response, an attempt to reveal the state of mind that exists in that 'moment of extreme pause' experienced by Tom Mathieson; that moment in which 'the veil which divides being and not-being becomes filmy, verges on becoming translucent'. Peter Munro's quest for the well at the world's end is a quest for precisely this state of mind, and for a way of life which is positive without being aggressive, flexible and responsive to changing circumstances. In essence it is a quest for creativity.

> Where most novels of the more ambitious kind today deal with violence and materialism leading to negation or despair, I thought it might be a change if I got a character who would wander among his fellows looking for the positive aspects of life. Is it possible to pierce the negative husk, the dark cloud, even for a few moments, and come on the light, the bubbling well at the end of the fairy tale? Do folk still do it, ordinary people? Can this feeling be conveyed, the moment of wonder, of integration? Not in any highfalutin or mystical way (I don't think I use the word mystical once) but close down to the earth among human happenings of a credible kind . . . And not as a thesis, but as something felt by the way, so that when it is quite forgotten it is still implicit. . . . And it must be carried through in the spirit of comedy because of a gaiety at the heart of the notion.[1]

105

Of all Gunn's novels, it is perhaps *The Well at the World's End* that comes closest to being a 'celebration of the light'. In the quest for the well, light is a prominent symbol, and the book is executed with such a marvellous lightness of touch that it mirrors perfectly the freedom attained by the central character:

> . . . an intermingling of fantasy and fact which in retrospect achieved a realm of its own, a realm neither on the earth nor off it . . . like living in a paradox, but then twice in a hushed forest aisle Peter had the distinct glimmering of a notion that that was how or where we actually lived. And there were moments when it went beyond that. (p.160)

The book is an endless arabesque of intertwining character and incident, linking back over all of Gunn's novels, and all seen in the light of Peter's growing awareness of the interrelatedness of all things. The world of *The Well at the World's End* is one of constant change and movement 'where minutes have no meaning; flash and colour and movement, and life itself lost in its own whirls'. (p.23) In this world inanimate objects spring to life: tombstones lift their heads; tall grasses laugh their heads off, and the whole natural world is apprehended as being alive. 'The trees grew, the grass was nibbled, the birds sang. A shoulder of rock hunched sideways over ferns.' (p.26) Everything in this world is seen with such vivid clarity that it seems to take on symbolic meaning. It is a world in which man is able to see through the apparent solidity of creatures and objects. 'Then he sank and floated and for a moment had a widening vision of Phemie's cat on the edge of the roof, its eyes closed in the morning sun, its whiskers at rest, and the trout inside.' (p.56) The quest for the well at the world's end is a process of learning to be at home in this 'other landscape', this bright, irrational world of delight.

The move on to the other landscape occurs right at the beginning, giving clear warning to the reader that this novel is to be concerned with levels of reality beyond the everyday. Not that this means an evasion of ordinary experience. Rather, the whole business of the quest is to explore those moments in which it is possible to glimpse the extraordinary qualities of the most ordinary happening. Thus the novel opens with an incident that actually happened to Neil Gunn while on holiday with his wife, Daisy, and it is to this autobiographical element that Stewart Conn refers when he describes the book as the most 'intimate and self-revealing' of all Gunn's novels.[2]

In the world of the novel it is Peter Munro, Professor of Ancient History, and his wife Fand, who are holidaying in the Highlands. Stopping at a cottage for water, they are directed by an old woman to her well. They find the well empty and cannot understand the old woman's apparent deception. Peter goes back to the woman and tells her that the well is dry. The old woman does not argue. She tells him simply, 'That well is never dry'. Peter, the academic, is set to argue this logically and rationally. But the woman, wise, and, by her very nature, beyond the futilities of argument, only smiles and corrects him. Peter, still trying to reason the business out in his mind, returns by the same path to the same well, only to discover that there *is* water in it. 'At first I laughed. That there should have been water in the well when we were so certain it was dry! Water so clear we thought it wasn't there!' (p.10) This is modern, rational, man face to face with the irrational—the Wise Old Woman of legend and fairy-tale, the water which isn't there and then suddenly *is*—and the shock of the experience awakens Peter to the possibility of positive value in this irrational element in life.

The encounter sets Peter off on his quest for 'the well at the world's end', the quest for the irrational 'something' that gives life meaning and value. 'That extraordinary moment when the invisible water moves in the well—is it as rare as all that? Do people, ordinary folk, ever stand tranced before some wonder that not only takes their breath away, but, for an instant, the human boundary itself away?' (p.20) This is the thought that motivates the quest. But it is made clear that such insight is gained only by the exercise of a higher form of awareness than conscious thought. As Peter and Fand climb a hill behind the Picts' houses, they find themselves suddenly in a strange new world.

107

> Then the drums started, the drumming of the snipe.
>
> The crest was further away than it had looked, but they reached it and found it not a crest but a tableland. They had come up into a higher dimension with a wider field for the eye. The birds were left behind, but suddenly [Fand] stood very still and, hearkening with her, he heard, far away and high in the air, the faint drumming of a last snipe. (p.16)

The action of the novel takes place in this 'higher dimension' of awareness, as Peter sets out to explore all the world's illusions in the attempt to discover 'that which we have the illusion about'. This means leaving behind the restrictions of conscious thought and encountering the world directly, recognising it as the spontaneous process that it is. And this is clearly linked to Peter's love for Fand. 'Moments like these still came upon them, as though they were strangers about to make intimate and lasting discoveries. Yet because of the discoveries they had made, the momentary experience when it came lay beyond love and the last intimacy in a place where they met in a new and strange relationship.' (p.17)

One answer to Peter's quest will be renewed understanding of this relationship. In a sense Peter's wife is the well he is seeking; and just as he had earlier been unable to see the water in an old woman's well, so he had been unable to grasp fully the mystery of his wife and his love for her. Among other things, then, *The Well at the World's End* is a love story; but the love discovered is much more comprehensive and all-embracing than the selfish desires we normally consider to be love.

The description of Peter and Fand's capture of the salmon— Gunn's favourite symbol of sexual awareness and of wisdom— is an image of the richness of their married life, as Peter realises when musing on Fand's inventiveness in stopping the fish: 'he was caught beyond laughter into the silent wonder that is pure delight. It was a revelation of another kind of thought, and he knew once again that in all the profound issues of life she could be trusted.' (p.23) The link between Fand and the well is one that is in Peter's mind throughout his journey, although it is not until the end of that journey that he is fully able to understand this. The link is made concrete to the reader by the fusion of light and water imagery with which Fand is consistently described: 'She had the innocence of a river or, more precisely, a Water, that dams wouldn't stop; so strong-willed and pertinacious and irrelevant that flowers came and grew on her banks.' (p.35)

Water and light are connected in Peter's mind in trying to work out how the well that appeared to be empty can suddenly be seen as being full—'that extraordinary moment when the invisible water moves in the well'. Light determines what we see although we cannot see light itself. This is also the symbolic function of the well; to find the well is to find that through which and in which we live, but which is beyond our rational comprehension as an object of knowledge. Fand, portrayed as the intuitive, irrational female, is alive to the nature of light and for her the world is not something to be understood intellectually, but something experienced directly. The world as she sees it is the world of light and delight which has so far eluded Peter. Fand not only sees things in this light but she is playfully aware of the faculty. 'She was looking at a round fleck of light on her wrist. She opened her long bony hand and drew it back until the fleck lay on her palm. Slowly she began to close her fingers, then snapped them shut, but the sunbeam danced onto her knuckles.' (p.11) The light is elusive, and cannot be consciously grasped. Understanding, as Fand is fully aware, will only come when one approaches it directly, without the limiting effect of conceptual thought.

In this attitude of 'no-mind' the dualistic sense of separation from the world disappears, and man experiences the freedom and delight inherent in being part of Tao. And in a work which quotes approvingly Chuang Tsu's injunction, 'Be empty', it is possible to see Peter as some kind of wandering Taoist sage.

> Quite suddenly he had the actual feeling of being on . . . holiday from himself, and the delightful sensation of freedom pervaded him. In this freedom he found he could not only look at people in the new expectant way, he could also look at trees and wild roses and running water. (p.20–1)

Both the idea and the natural imagery through which it is expressed hint at the essentially Taoist flavour of Peter's quest.

The quest for the well requires Peter to give up conceptual thought because it is one of the principal ways in which the illusion of man's separate and fixed ego is built up and maintained. This, as Peter recognises, is not only a futile waste of time and energy, but also potentially destructive: 'man has got to that condition . . . that when he has no one else to argue with he argues with himself. Man is the serpent who sucks his own tail.' (p.55) By ending the distracting 'chatter' of conceptual thought, through what the East recognises as meditation, man gradually becomes aware of the world as a realm of infinite creativity.

The first and most important step is the avoidance of the channels of conditioned thought: 'Give up learning and put an end to your troubles,' says Lao Tsu.[3]

> He had had the brilliant idea of liberating himself from all paths, though if a path came his way he would not necessarily disdain it. But he would not be conditioned by the human path . . . If there was one thing he had made a vow to avoid it was thought. (p.32)

Bearing in mind that this statement itself is conceptual, how is this state beyond thought to be reached? No amount of analysis can help here. The answer is simply to let it happen. There is no way that 'I' can become aware of 'myself meditating', as this would only perpetuate the split between the first and second selves. The mind must simply realise that there is no way it can be learned through conscious effort, until, in that moment of defeat, one realises that it just happens, quite simply, of itself. It is as natural as breathing. Indeed, in many schools of meditation 'watching the breath' is the starting point. Gradually the forced attention of watching the breath gives way to a quiet awareness of the process of breathing happening 'of itself' (*tzu-jan*), with no need for conscious effort:

> '. . . the breath coming and going on its own—as if it were falling out and falling in, not as being pushed out or pulled in.
> In the same spirit, one does not listen, but simply hears all sounds that are emerging from silence without making any effort

110

to place or identify them. Similarly, one does not look, but only sees light, color, and form playing with the eyes as they, too, emerge moment by moment from the void. Thoughts, likewise are treated in the same way as sounds, and, if they arise, are merely watched without comment as they come and go; one 'hears' them in the same way one would hear the chattering of birds on the roof.[4]

This detached but responsive attitude comes also to Peter Munro in *The Well at the World's End*: 'he was in that delightful condition of mind which recognises thought as no more than the scent of the flower. He could sniff it when he liked.' (p.52)

The book's characteristic tone of playful humour reflects this same detached attitude of mind—an attitude of mind which is prepared to take things as they come and not to take oneself too seriously, not to force issues. As Peter himself acknowledges, his quest is light and playful rather than heavy and argumentative. Critics who do not recognise this have missed the whole point of the book. The plot, such as it is, is utterly preposterous —a Professor of Ancient History giving up a well-earned holiday with his wife to indulge in a fairy-tale quest for something he knows he will never find! And no one is quicker to see the joke than the Professor himself. He laughs at himself continuously, appalled at taking himself so seriously, fully aware of the Quixotic nature of his quest.

It is a humour which breaks through in even the most serious moments. Right at the beginning of his journey Peter is almost defeated by a rock climb that stretches him to the limits. While engaged in this perilous undertaking, however, fear and humour in equal measure are his protectors. This balance of emotions gives him the capacity to endure.

This light-hearted, playful approach to the problematic business of living is also characteristic of Zen and of Taoism as Suzuki points out in his introduction to a book of paintings and drawings by Zen master Sengai. Here Suzuki emphasises the essential humour of Sengai's work, and relates this to his mastery of Zen.

Sengai's transcendentalism comes from his Zen, and his humorous playfulness too. When one sees directly into ultimate reality

111

and can survey the world of relativities from this angle he feels a sense of detachment toward things around him; detachment because they are all seen as passing in time. When this contemplation is transferred into the inwardness of things it is the feeling of *myo*, wonder. *Myo* (*miao* in Chinese) is a difficult term to translate. And this *myo* has an aspect of playfulness which is not merely amusement; it is accompanied with a sense of mystery or magic which is altogether entrancing.[5]

This is close to Gunn's sense of 'the warm mystery in natural living' which informs the whole of *The Well at the World's End*, and which is possibly seen at its clearest in his description of Peter's meeting with old Phemie Bethune.

An old woman living alone in her cluttered cottage which Peter sees as the half-way house between heaven and earth, Phemie lives in the midst of domestic chaos. But this, as Peter realises, is her Way.

> She was so old that she wasn't shy, only flustered. As he looked round the little kitchen, at the wooden boxed bed against the wall with its patchwork quilt, at the clutter about the clay floor and the traces of adventurous hens, at the smoke-grimed wall-paper hanging in a torn bulge over the bed, at the table beside his right shoulder and before the window on which everything unwashed was hardly given standing room, he realised that the kitchen and the things outside were like herself and that they all lived together.

The description of the cottage, with its patchwork quilt, the hens, the table covered with crockery, although faithful to Highland cottages is more reminiscent of the fairy-tale cottages of childhood's books. This is deliberate and links Phemie with the old woman whose well had set Peter off on his quest. But Phemie is no witch from a fairy-tale. Like Mairi in *Butcher's Broom* she is the embodiment of a traditional way of life, which retains its awareness of the Way which underlies all other paths.

Peter's meeting with Phemie is only one of many such encounters, all of which allow him some insight into the magical quality of life when experienced in its totality. His involvement in each of these situations reflects and interacts

112

with all the others so that his awareness is never static but is always changing, always responsive to that which is happening *at that very moment*. Each of these encounters is like a Zen *koan*, one of those unanswerable questions Zen masters set their students. As Peter becomes more and more involved in a region where logical analysis is not enough to produce understanding, his responsiveness to this region's own inner logic is a measure of his growing awareness.

The idea of the *koan* in Zen is that the master sets his student a question that cannot be answered by the exercise of logic alone, so forcing the student to discover within himself the ability to apprehend the world directly and intuitively, through the exercise of *prajñā*, or transcendental wisdom. There are many different kinds of *koan*, but the object of the exercise is always this driving of the student out of the limitations of logic. For example, the master might ask, 'What is the sound of one hand?' Or the question might be posed in relation to an incident which the master outlines: 'A man is hanging over an abyss by his teeth. Someone asks him why Bodhidharma came to China. If he does not answer he fails. If he does answer he falls. What should he do?'[6] To the uninitiated such questions seem bizarre and totally nonsensical. This in fact is their whole purpose. Although there *are* recognised answers to the *koans* which one can learn and then reproduce, this is not important. What is important is the state of mind which working on the *koan*, over a considerable period of time, engenders in the student. The constant presence of the *koan* in his mind helps to develop a state of receptivity which will recognise Enlightenment when it comes. Enlightenment will only come when the unnecessary machinations of thought have been stilled, and the *koan* exercise brings this about in different ways to fit different kinds of student.

The particular emphasis placed on the *koan* in Rinzai Zen stems from the belief that it is a genuine method of teaching by no-method. A *koan* can be one of the traditional kind or, as used always to be the case, it can arise naturally out of a student's discussions with the master. Anything can form the basis of a *koan*, as long as the master is fully aware of the way any

113

particular student's mind works so that he can set as his *koan* a problem which will have a unique resonance in the mind of that student. As with the teaching methods of the Sufis, it is a process which becomes inseparable from the rest of one's life. There can be no evasion; the problem has to be worked through.

This process of 'working through' a problem is the way the healthy mind naturally deals with problems or setbacks. In the case of the student of Zen, however, the mind is no longer healthy. It is beset by all sorts of desires, and particularly by the desire for Enlightenment. Such desires commit the very mistake the student is trying to stop making—the mistake of considering that there is a separate 'self' which can seek 'Enlightenment'. Mr Gwynn, in *The Key of the Chest* puts it succinctly: 'At some moment when I try to achieve a harmony within me, the tail of my inner eye will see that Buddha, and harmony will be split.' (p.175)

Working on the *koan* forces the student beyond this superficial separation of the knower and known by awakening in him the capacity to 'see' the world with the meditative mind. Knowledge then becomes a function of his whole being and not just a matter of the intellect. When this stage is reached the world is apprehended with vivid intensity.

> If a person is able to see the energies of the universe as they are, then shapes and colors and patterns suggest themselves; symbolism happens. That is the meaning of *mahāmudra*, which means 'great symbol'. The whole world is symbol—not symbol in the sense of a sign representing something other than itself, but symbol in the sense of the highlights of the vivid qualities of things as they are.[7]

It is through this symbolic world that Peter wanders, seeking the answer to his own *koan*: how can one find the well at the world's end? Each incident on his quest serves to clarify and expand his awareness of the nature of his quest. Each episode interacts with and echoes all the others, bringing him closer to understanding what it all means. For the reader there is the additional interaction of character, setting and incident with similar characters, settings and incidents in earlier novels, giving an added resonance to Peter's quest.

In some ways the quest seems undisciplined, and rather aimless. But this is to be expected as it is a quest into the unknown, a moving away from the security of conceptual thought. What is undertaken is a direct confrontation of the world in all its confusion and variety. It is in the nature of such a quest that there can be no aim, no discipline, in the sense of conscious control. One is totally involved in a process which is infinitely greater than the conscious ego's conception of what is or should be. All one can do is to remain open and responsive; 'Be aware of all that is and dwell in the infinite', says Chuang Tsu.[8] This may sound like a dangerous giving in to the forces of the unconscious, as in a sense it is, but it must be remembered that such an undertaking is only entered on by those who are ready for it. Once the process is begun, one moves gradually towards Enlightenment. In his *Zen and Zen Classics* R. H. Blyth quotes Kankei's description of this process:

> 'When I was with Rinzai I got a ladleful, and when I was with Massan a ladleful.' He added, 'It is all open and unhidden in the ten directions, not a gate on the four sides, completely clear, without any attachment to anything at all, no place to take hold of it.'

Blyth comments: 'This is one of the best definitions of Zen. We get a ladleful of it here and there according to our (accidental) innate abilities, and our (accidental) opportunities.'[9]

In *The Well at the World's End* Peter Munro gets one of his 'ladlefuls' when he stumbles on a cave where whisky is being secretly distilled by three local men: Jock, Alick, and Hamish. And once it has been established that Peter has no connection with the Customs and Excise Department he is accepted by the men, who reveal to him something of their art. They offer him some whisky, which he accepts, thus forming a bond of communion between himself and these distillers of the spirit.

In the cave talk becomes extravagant and fanciful, as the talk of men who have been drinking tends to be. But as in MacDiarmid's poem about a drunk man this extravagance is intended to be seen as a positive quality of vision—a pushing

115

beyond the boundary of the known. The cave is a traditional symbol of the unconscious, so the extravagance of the talk is intended to convey something of the wonder of the other landscape itself.

The whisky which Peter drinks immediately rejuvenates him—it is, after all, 'the water of life'—and is clearly linked with his quest for the well.

> Peter was now aware of having recovered in a remarkable manner. Even the ache in his head had dissolved, as in a burning quicksilver, and left in its place a wonderful clarity, a delightful lightness. He looked into the cup and couldn't see the liquor . . . as once upon a time he hadn't been able to see the water in an old wife's well. (p.118)

It is in the light of this 'wonderful clarity' that the talk turns to discussion of Peter's quest, and both Jock and Alick relate their own experiences of 'going through the boundary' and penetrating the unknown. Their stories are very different—one humorous, the other more serious—but both add something to Peter's understanding.

Jock tells how he had once ruined some whisky he was distilling because of an encounter with an enchantress. The hum of the boiling pot had lulled him to sleep and he had dreamed of a meeting with a tall, fair-haired woman, whom Peter is able to identify as the Fand of Celtic legend. Lost in his dream, Jock had let the whisky go to ruin so that his encounter with the other landscape, although memorable, had not been productive.

Alick also has had an encounter with the other landscape. He had once narrowly escaped drowning while on holiday in Spain, and the following morning, standing at his hotel window, he had caught a glimpse of this other world.

> When I awoke the dawn was in the window. It was a tall window. Immediately I was wide awake, with a pleasant feeling of lightness . . . I got up and went to the window, and found myself looking out on an old Spanish garden. The dawn was quite clear but there was as yet no sign of the sun, only the freshness of the morning. The garden was very still. Stone walls, architectural

lines, the shoulder of a building . . . the whole was somehow arranged to hold this stillness . . . Then I saw that the stillness went out beyond the garden; and I held my breath in an effort to catch the suggestion of an utmost sound. But there was no sound. It was now that the odd feeling came over me that the stillness itself was holding something, much as the walls held the garden; and in a moment I realised that what it was holding was time. Time was stopped, not by any kind of magic or enchantment, but actually . . . Quite simply, then, I knew with an absolute conviction as I stood at that window gazing out on the old Spanish garden that there exists an order of things outside our conception of time . . . The moment—however long it lasted—was one of absolute impersonality . . . (pp.147–8)

Jock had gained something from his encounter, and had laughed at his human frailty. For Alick, however, the moment had passed and left him empty, unable to regain the 'delicious humour' of the experience. This has engendered in him a sense of conflict and anxiety by emphasising the separation between himself and what he now knows to be the real world, the world beyond the boundary of thought. Unable to give up thought— Alick, it is emphasised, has had a university education—he is unable to pass freely beyond that boundary; he has not, like Peter, 'learned the trick of it'. And throughout his own journey Peter is troubled by a vision of Alick lost in the 'deserts of the intellect', 'tortured by the arid unbelief that dogs and withers'. Alick's story serves to highlight Peter's own. Hampered by thought, Alick is caught up in conflict which he is unable to work through while Peter, on the other hand, is able to leave thought behind and enter freely into the landscape of freedom and delight.

And this movement beyond thought is a positive movement in that it leads to freedom, not freedom *from* something, but freedom itself, which is the natural state of things before duality arises. In *The Well at the World's End*, this is suggested most strongly by the imagery of expansiveness and light which marks Peter's growing sense of self-awareness, and the way in which this is linked through similar imagery to renewed awareness of his love for his wife, Fand.

117

The reawakening of love's spontaneity is one of the book's main themes, examined also in the story of Mrs Douglas and her husband, guests at a hotel in which Peter stays at one point:

> . . . he divined that Douglas and his wife had been married for ten or twelve years and that in the mysterious interactions of things she, at this particular pass in their wedded bliss, couldn't do anything right in his sight. There was no known cure for this condition while it lasted, which might be quite a long time. Worst of it was that the more the woman tried to do the right thing the more wrong it was. (p.187)

Peter overhears Mrs Douglas talking to a ghillie about a plant which has the property of restoring virtue. Later the minister explains the properties of this particular plant, called in Gaelic *mothan*, which is sometimes used as a love potion, a fact that interests Mrs Douglas, particularly when the minister mentions that the plant is only to be found in one place in the area—the western slope of the hill above Loch a' Cheo. The 'virtue' the plant can restore is that which gives something value, its 'substance and goodness' as the minister puts it. It is that indefinable quality that gives life value and meaning. In Peter's terms it is the well at the world's end—that which is rarely consciously appreciated, but which is missed as soon as it is absent. To the Taoists, this quality is known as *Te*: 'the unthinkable ingenuity and creative power of man's spontaneous and natural functioning—a power which is blocked when one tries to master it in terms of formal methods and techniques'.[10] *Te* is the natural goodness in life which we obscure by thought. For Mrs Douglas this means both her spontaneity, and the spontaneity of her marriage. It is the recovery of this naturalness and spontaneity which Peter is privileged to see, in another episode which nudges the reader on to the other landscape with its suggestions of folk-tale and the supernatural.

On a damp misty night above Loch a' Cheo, Peter watches Mrs Douglas searching for the magical plant, a quest which 'exposed the human condition. It was neither pitiful nor childish, it was stark'. While watching her, he becomes aware of another figure emerging from the mist. It is the woman's husband, who has followed her. In the clash that follows Douglas accuses his wife of having an affair with Peter's friend Cocklebuster, a suggestion so absurd that it is clearly an invention of his own to give some definite reason for the estrangement between him and his wife. He is still trapped in the realm of thought, unable to accept the irrational aspects of life, always seeking reasons and causes. But Mrs Douglas reacts to his accusation in such a spontaneously irrational fashion that this breaks the deadlock and allows both of them to break through to a different level of perception. This action is the administering of the love potion. And when Peter sees the couple later on that day it is clear that this traditional cure has worked, has healed the split in their relationship. The substance, the virtue which they thought had been lost has been found again, just as a change in perspective had revealed the water in the old woman's well. The whole episode gives Peter a deeper awareness of the meaning of love. Always love is beyond thought. It can never be pinned down by explanations, can never be fixed, because the experience of love is the experience of freedom.

This renewed awareness of the nature of love is clearly linked to his own relationship with Fand through the character of Peggy, the hotel chambermaid. Peggy is Fand as she was at nineteen, and Peter's infatuation with her is a renewal of his infatuation with Fand when he had first met her, and is a clear indication of the direction he must take to end his quest. His quest will end where it began, with Fand. But before he can return to her he must pass a final test. He has found the well he is seeking by realising that it can only be reached by learning to live beyond thought. But even this insight is still within the realm of thought. To end his quest he must go beyond even this, must face an absolute dissolution of thought.

The ending of the book describes Peter's descent into darkness, and his winning through to the light. After being witness to a remarkable feat of seamanship and a unique act of humanity, Peter goes on his way, feeling that with this glimpse of man's nobility his quest is ended. In fact the climax of his quest has still to be reached. Gradually the scene darkens, both literally and metaphorically. Peter realises that he will hardly be able to return to Fand until after nightfall and he becomes troubled, feeling that there might still be something he has to do.

The crucial feature in this last section of the quest is the reappearance of thought to disrupt his secure sense of success. As in *Highland River* the actuality of nearing the source is obscured by thinking about it. Thought weaves its own webs, as Peter well knows, but he has still to learn to handle them. 'He stretched himself flat out by the loch. Why should he hurry? The only real appointment man had was with death. That would come soon enough. No need of rushing towards it, or thinking about it. Then he began to think about it. . . .' (p.263) This is the intrusion of the calculating ego, afraid for its own safety. Its grip is finally broken by Peter's attempt to save a lamb which has managed to get itself trapped over the edge of a cliff.

Having seen the lamb, Peter is troubled as to whether or not he should try to rescue it. All kinds of excuses present themselves to him. This is thought asserting itself. But he knows that the correct action in the circumstances is for him to save the lamb, however foolhardy the attempt might be. It is simply something he must do. In a way, he has made this into his *koan*, and he knows that he will have no peace until he does try to rescue it, whatever the outcome. The dilemma is focussed in the reappearance in Peter's mind of a goat which had earlier taunted him, an animal which represents the machinations of conscious thought. And the need, as Peter recognises, is for action not for thought. 'All this turning and twisting, this indecision, was draining his substance. Even his use of the goat was but a way of dodging the direct look at the terrible act.' (p.269) Caught up in the webs of inconsequential thought a 'sensation of profound desolation' overtakes him, until he decides to act. But the attempt to save the lamb fails, and Peter is knocked unconscious in the fall down the cliff-face. He regains consciousness in darkness, and in great pain.

He finds himself, then, near the end of his journey, lying injured at the bottom of a cliff, with no food and getting weaker all the time. This time there is no certainty of survival. At this point, alone on the hill, with the ravens feeding on the body of the lamb and the hoodie crow circling overhead, among these images of desolation, Peter fights for survival, and for the knowledge of the validity of his quest. He is alone with all the hopes and fears to which man is subject, his capacity for decisive action seriously impaired.

But during his quest Peter has learned a wisdom that transcends such fears and gives him the capacity to conserve his energy and to protect his vital centre, his second self. The second self is different from the first self, the ego, as it is not a construct of thought and does not function as a result of thought. And it instinctively knows how to protect itself. 'The sick brute curls into itself, comes to rest secure in the centre of itself. It is cunning, it knows what is waiting to pounce on it. But within the circle it can lie secure, and the sun lies with it.' (p.273) Circle and centre, with the self in the centre of the circle. This is the *mandala* symbol of psychic integration. Peter's ability to protect his centre is an instinctive application of the principle of the *mandala* as an aid to psychic survival and growth. The extreme circumstances in which he finds himself ensures that this is not a concept but a reality. It is this reality that Peter must learn to accept. And this he does by exhausting the possibilities of thought. By giving in to all the fluctuations of his mind he is able to see them as empty gestures, and so is able to grasp the reality which underlies all the fluctuations.

In this he is aided by 'the wild man', a man who, like himself, had given up the pressures of living in society, but who had done so permanently, now living rough on the moors and in the hills. From the beginning, Peter had recognised an affinity with this man, sensing that he is driven by the same compulsion as himself—the desire for freedom. Now, at the end of his quest, he comes on a cave which he is certain must be one of the wild man's sanctuaries and, in his weakened condition, decides to shelter there for the night. At the back of his mind is the hope that the wild man will find him in the cave and bring help. And during the night Peter is woken by the feeling that someone has come in to the cave. He is convinced that this is the wild man, although he can neither see nor hear anyone. It is only later that he discovers that the wild man had been found dead shortly before his own arrival in the cave; 'he had fallen over a cliff in the neighbourhood of the cave where he usually slept'. All along Peter has been aware of the wild man as an image of the ideal to which he aspired. But the reality of this is very different from the ideal. There is nothing romantic about the night Peter spends in the wild man's cave, cold, and delirious through pain and hunger. The experience of becoming one with the wild man is traumatic as it means coming to terms with all of his own fears, but this is necessary if the experience is to be meaningful, and not simply an evasion of social responsibility.

Peter's descent into the darkness of himself, then, is the necessary prelude to his living in the light of freedom, and throughout the last section of the novel the idea of spiritual desolation is counterpointed by glimpses of the light which symbolise the awakening into a new realm of consciousness, the moment Zen Buddhists call *satori*. Going over his journey in his mind Peter becomes more aware of its meaning and significance, not as a concept but as a reality. This new awareness is experienced as a sense of lightness and expansiveness which is recognisable as an intimation of the way he must go. 'But the thought of philosophic systems grew heavy as always. And at least a man could get out of an enclosed system as out of a cave, by going into the light.' Feelings of bodily lightness and glimpses of the light of wisdom are all Peter has to guide him in this last part of his quest. Finally they come together in the experience of Enlightenment itself. And it is fitting that Gunn, who had used the salmon and the deer in *Highland River* as emblematic of this experience, should once again use the image of a magical beast to suggest the wonder of it.

Trapped, weak and injured, in the cave Peter sees, in his delirium, a lion lying on the threshold, barring his way out.

> Now he was in an appalling dilemma; he might be able to hide in the cave . . . die in the cave . . . but he would never get out unless he got past the lion. The black walls sweated their dampness upon

him. the decision sweated agony out of him, but he made it; he crawled forward, in a sickness of terror he went on; the lion's head lifted but looked into the country of light and its growl was a hollow roar that ended abruptly as its mouth closed. Its tail switched; the golden skin rippled over the upthrust of the haunches . . . Peter wanted to speak to the lion, to placate the beast, but his mouth clove against all sound. In the end, in the end, he lifted a hand to put it on the lion's back; the lion twitched and roared like a great beast in a game; Peter got up and was stepping over the lion when he awoke.

He saw the golden hide of that beast for a long time, and he saw the light in the country beyond. (p.290)

All of Peter's quest is contained here. He is trapped in 'the cave of his mind' in the darkness of his ego, tortured by phantasms, and unable to reach the other landscape of freedom and delight beyond the cave. The entrance to that world is guarded by the most ferocious of the phantasms, thought, here symbolised by the lion. To reach the other landscape man must learn to deal with thought, must conquer fear which is caused by the limitations of thought.

The book's last chapter sees the ending of Peter's quest in his return to Fand, who had been there, implicitly, all along. On one level Fand is the feminine, intuitive aspect of Peter's psyche so that his reunion with her is a symbol of psychic integration, of the acknowledgement of the importance of this less conscious side of himself. But she is more than symbol. She is the wife he loves profoundly. And in the darkness of introspection in the final stages of his quest his love for her has been reawakened in all its original intensity. Freed from the habits of thought, his vision of her is no longer restricted, and he is able to feel the love between them as a creative force; never static, but always developing and growing in depth and understanding. This is conveyed by a vision of Fand which echoes Aodhagán Ó Rathaille's remarkable *aisling* poem, 'Gile na Gile' ('Brightness of Brightness') in its picture of woman as an intensity of light.

A light now was in the lightness round his head, and in this light the tenderness that was the core of her being rose like a spring, like a springing fountain, and was crystal as the well from which a man could drink and be strengthened . . .

And at last he knew that this was the ultimate vision, that this was what remained and rose up when time and chance had done their best and worst, through the deceits and faithlessness of the mortal flesh, and withered away. Here, the bravery and the brightness, the light from her eyes . . . (pp.291–2)

In coming back to Fand Peter's quest has come full circle, has returned to the source. As the Zen masters have said this is the way understanding grows.

Before I had studied Zen for thirty years, I saw mountains as mountains, and waters as waters. When I arrived at a more intimate knowledge, I came to the point where I saw that mountains are not mountains and waters are not waters. But now that I have got its very substance I am at rest. For it's just that I see mountains once again as mountains, and waters once again as waters.[11]

The difference lies in the loss of that self-importance that obtruded between Peter and the world, preventing him from seeing. Once this is realised, he is ready to begin the journey again. Only this time he is more aware of the nature of the path he is taking. Now there is no need for talk of transcendence. The affair is simple and straightforward, and irradiated with the wonder that recognises the movement of life itself.

That's the way it went . . . the way.

No one could see the end of the way, but of the way itself, in insight, in understanding, there could be no doubt. For man could experience that, and know its relief, and know its strange extended gladness.

That was the beginning . . . If the lure of transcendence, of timeless or immortal implication, came around, pay no great attention, but move from one step to the next, and look at this face and stay with that . . . and let what would happen in the place where happenings and boundaries were. (p.294)

BEYOND VIOLENCE
Bloodhunt 1952

The Well at the World's End traces the awakening in man of a creative response to life, and the book's light and playful tone celebrates the attainment of such a wisdom. Because of this it would have made a fitting last novel, but Gunn was not content to leave the matter there. His next novel, *Bloodhunt* (1952), is concerned with the problem of how such a creative, non-violent attitude can be maintained in the face of the increasing violence of the modern world. With its stark opposition of creative and destructive responses to experience, the novel is concerned to show how the creative will always prevail, because it is based on a reality greater than man. Creativity is the 'Way' of Tao. But in *Bloodhunt* Gunn seeks to show that although the creative attitude will always prevail, it does not do so easily, or without loss. Indeed it seems to be equally in the way of things that the adoption of such an attitude to experience makes man particularly vulnerable, and in the story of old Sandy Grant, Gunn shows how man must learn to live with this vulnerability, as this is the only way in which creativity will be preserved.

But it is not only the external violence of the world that undermines the creative attitude. It is also attacked from within in the form of self-doubt and fear; fear of that vulnerability or openness to experience which is a measure of man's understanding. Having caught sight of the 'Way', it is easy for man to think he is disinterestedly following it by withdrawing from the everyday problems which surround him. But the detachment advocated by Zen and Taoism implies a full and continual

125

involvement in life, because only when involvement is complete will wholeness be attained and detachment understood. For detachment is not the avoidance of experience, but the ability to live without insisting on the importance of the ego. Ultimately such an attitude awakens one to the interconnectedness of all things, and leads to the attainment of wisdom and through this to the other great Mahāyāna Buddhist virtue of compassion. *Bloodhunt* is much more than the 'thriller' its title suggests: it is an investigation of the interaction of wisdom and compassion.

In *Bloodhunt* the dichotomy between the creative and the destructive elements in man are explored in a story which is structured round one of Gunn's favourite motifs—the hunt. The hunt had a particular fascination for Gunn as participation in the hunt affords man the opportunity of seeing himself in a different, a more elemental light. Participation in such a basic activity makes man more aware of essentials, and exposes his true nature. For some, the experience of the hunt is liberating and expansive, and the hunt becomes as in *Highland River*, a 'poaching expedition to the source of delight'. But for others, such as Geoffrey in *Second Sight*, participation in the hunt serves only to highlight his alienation from the world, an alienation that results in destruction. It is this condition that is exposed by the hunt in *Bloodhunt*:

> They were after the murderer. They were on the old blood hunt. The satisfaction of the final kill.
> More and more . . . nearer and nearer . . . violence upon violence, increasing violence . . . until the teeth champed and the juices ran about the gums . . . Then satisfaction, the satisfaction after the orgy . . . until the hunt did not need a murderer, could substitute something else, an-*ism* or-*ology* that stood for the murderer, providing a wider hunt, a greater kill, more blood . . . (p.99)

Like many modern novels *Bloodhunt* is concerned with the problem of violence, but its most interesting feature is the way in which it suggests a positive response to the problem; man cannot pretend that violence does not exist but he can grow to understand and so control it.

The storyline of the novel is simple and uncluttered, centring round the hunt for a murderer in a small Highland community. Allan Innes has murdered Robert Nicol in a quarrel over the girl Liz Murison who is pregnant by Nicol. A manhunt is quickly organised to catch the murderer and it is led by the local policeman, the murdered man's brother. An elderly crofter, Sandy Grant, shields Allan from the police, and later gives shelter to Liz Murison who has left her own home. Tension is generated by Sandy's efforts to protect Allan from Nicol—even when he is himself injured and confined to bed for a few days. And while Sandy is unsure as to his motives and as to the rightness of his action in protecting the young man, Nicol the policeman becomes gradually more and more obsessed with the hunt for his brother's killer—to the extent that he has to be relieved of his duties. The novel ends with Sandy as witness to Allan's death at the hands of Nicol on the moor where he had been hiding, and deciding that in some primitive way justice has worked itself out. He does not report what he has seen as that would lead only to further violence in a court case against Nicol, and possibly in a hanging. As an old man, Sandy has seen enough futile violence, and so he takes upon himself the burden of responsibility. Having accepted that burden, he turns himself to looking after Liz and her child, and so the novel of violence and destruction ends with a traditional symbol of love's creativity—a mother and her child. 'Liz Murison was crooning an old Highland lullaby to her child. He had never heard her sing before. The tune seemed to well up from his own roots for it had put him to sleep many a time. Her voice was warm and the lullaby full of a woman's knowledge.' (pp.249–50)

The real focus of the novel, though, is not the hunt itself, but Sandy's attempts to understand it. Two other, rejected, titles for the novel show this clearly: 'Eyes of Mercy', and 'Goodness Knows.' But the focus on Sandy as the novel's centre is apparent to any perceptive reader. The real action of *Bloodhunt* is not the obvious external business of the hunt, but rather Sandy's own inner struggle to understand both the violence and his own response to it. Sandy's croft is the physical centre

127

of most of the action. The book opens with Nicol searching the croft for Allan who is known to be a friend of the old man's. Later, Allan comes to the croft for food, and it is to this same croft that Liz Murison comes for asylum. Here also her child is born and, beyond the immediate story, Sandy is to leave the croft to Liz and her son as security for the future. Just as the croft is the physical centre of the book Sandy himself is its spiritual centre. Most of the book's action is described to the reader as it is seen through his eyes.

And Sandy's perspective is valuable. Described at one point as 'a bit of a philospher' he is linked in the reader's mind with Tom Mathieson of *The Serpent* when the minister compares the movement of his mind in argument with the movement of a serpent through the heather. The old man living 'at the back of beyond' as one character puts it, is not simply an eccentric but is clearly intended to be seen as a man who has lived a full life and who has earned the right to live out his last years in contemplation of life's joys and absurdities. In this he is still very much a part of the community. He had known Allan Innes and several other young men through his involvement in their poaching activities, an activity which in Gunn's fiction is a ritual which binds men together. Living on the edge of the community, retaining an active involvement in it while devoting much of his time to contemplative meditation, he is regarded as something of a 'character' by his neighbours. 'In fact only in the last year or two had he realised that he was regarded as a "character". Folk repeated his "sayings", and occasionally made them up. This had come as a great surprise to him.' (p.22) And even in his most contemplative moments Sandy is clearly linked to the community. As an old man of seventy-four it is not surprising that his thoughts often revolve around the awareness that death cannot be far away.

> It had been one of Sandy's hopes that before the end he would find out if the spirit was immortal. Already he had had a remarkable experience about this.
>
> The country of the spirit had been gradually taking shape, gathering a feature here, a snapshot there, a certain light . . . but mostly when he wanted to catch a whole glimpse of it and enter its

mood, he only saw the hills, the lochs, the bracken, the birches
. . . This was the land he had come to . . . the bit of earth that
held his heart, the beautiful country . . . (p.30)

Like Dark Mairi in *Butcher's Broom* Sandy is a symbol of the
traditional wisdom of the community. His 'philosophy' is a final
distillation of the community's natural wisdom. 'His cheeks
were rounded and ruddy. There was a roundness in the slope
of his shoulders, too, as if time and thought had rounded off his
whole person into something final and matured. He was like a
fruit that had grown ripe after its kind, like a gathered apple
that keeps a long time.' (pp.16–17) And because wisdom cannot
be conceptualised and measured and often goes unrecognised
Sandy, like Mairi, quite often appears as stupid or stubborn to
observers. He shares Mairi's 'blankness' and 'vacancy' when
faced with certain kinds of thought, and to those minds which
handle such thought well, appears as quite ludicrous: 'Many
looked at his bushy face and old half-trotting body and laughed
as at something that had come out of a croft bog in its Sunday
clothes.' (p.26) But such thought is not beyond these embodi-
ments of wisdom, and at times Sandy sees himself in the same
way—'A useless futile kind of man if ever there was one'. His
wisdom lies in the ability to transcend such debilitating
thoughts and handle them with detachment. If there is no
identification with the sense of a permanent ego then it does
not matter whether one feels 'useless' or 'futile'. One continues
to act, and gradually it becomes clear that action on this level is
quite natural and spontaneous.

> Even now Sandy could not set his mind to work, make it
> overcome the strange reluctance he had experienced all along to
> think out the awful problem, with its tail-end of court trial and
> hanging. Extraordinary thing was that in the moment of emer-
> gency he acted with incredible cunning in order to mislead the law
> and shield Allan. This was done without any thought at all. (p.43)

And one of the most interesting features of Gunn's portrait of
him as the wise old man of the tribe concerns the way in which
Sandy is seen by others always to act on this level beyond
thought, while at the same time clearly revealing to the reader

the intensity of his inner struggle for understanding. Dealing with confused and frightened people he is obliged to remain calm and self-possessed, while in reality he is as confused and at times as frightened as anyone else. His external calmness helps to sustain the other characters, and helps Sandy himself to attain an inner calm and a quiet strength which gives him the power of endurance, an endurance linked to that of the community and of the land itself to which he is clearly linked. Falling asleep on the moor at one point, Sandy is seen to merge with the landscape. 'The felt hat tilted off his head. The bone of the skull, his hair, the skin on the hands, were old like the lichen, the moss, the runtled heather stalks.' (p.35)

Sandy's place in the community is further evidenced by the contrast Gunn draws between the old crofter and the minister. While Sandy is *in* and *of* the community in which he lives, the minister, by nature of his doctrinally-held position as a Christian, is an outsider in the community which he professes to guide towards a better life. Sandy and the minister are old friends, and it is the minister who reveals to him that Liz Murison is pregnant to Robert Nicol.

> The minister talked of the three families involved, the three mothers, the horror and the stigma, but Sandy hardly heard him. In the night he had worried over what could have driven Allan to the fatal act, and no passion from any love rivalry, he felt, could excuse him, no hot blood, no spite, no anger. But *this*—this in a moment took all questioning from Sandy and left him sitting dumb and still. (pp.23–24)

Mr Davidson, like the missionary in George Mackay Brown's story 'The Wireless Set', sees events in an external way—as things that happen *to* the community, not as things that happen *within* the community, a community in which he is directly involved. Sandy, as part of the community darkened by the murder of a young man, feels the effect of that shadow more deeply, more intimately, than the minister. Consequently, his final understanding of the nature and significance of the crime is greater than Mr Davidson's can ever be.

As the novel opens we see the effect of the murder of Robert Nicol on Sandy and, by extension, on the community as a whole. The peace and order of the old man's life are shattered by the intrusion of the policeman, a symbol of authority and a figure of menace. 'So great was the shock that Sandy's understanding seemed blinded by the darkness.' (p.9) Nicol searches the croft thoroughly, so thoroughly that Sandy finds it hard to keep sight of the human being behind the mask of authority.

Nicol climbs a ladder to the loft and, from his position at the foot of the ladder, Sandy sees him distorted by the angle and by the light of his small torch—dehumanised, but still performing his function as the manhunter. 'In the magical is a touch of the old primeval fear . . . Looked at from underneath, the policeman's features were also of that realm of fear and strangeness, foreshortened, bony, with the nose prominent and ominous as any hound's.' (p.17) Even so, Sandy is able to see beyond this horrific distortion to the equally horrific reality behind it; that it is not just the desire for justice that motivates this man, but the desire for revenge. When Nicol eventually leaves, Sandy is clearly upset, cannot quite grasp what has happened. This is the general mood of the community, but it is more sharply focussed in the picture of the old crofter whose peace of mind is destroyed by the intrusion of violence.

> Sandy shut the door and wandered back into the kitchen, where he stood staring at things he did not see. The force of the policeman's concentration, behind the cool talk, the restrained manner, kept him from being able to think. It was as pure a human force as he had met. The lack of haste had something terrifying about it.
>
> His legs tremored and brought him into the arm chair . . .
>
> The kettle sounded a low note and he got lost completely. He came back thinking there was nothing in the books which could deal with this kind of moment; nothing at all to dispel what came out of it, the awfulness of the human act. (p.19)

Sandy is deeply troubled, just as the community as a whole is deeply troubled, by the murder. He feels it directly, as something in which he is himself involved, and cannot externalise it as the minister can, not because he is too stupid but rather because he is able to see the futility of such a course.

131

His evasion of any coherent response to the event is a deliberate moral choice, made for reasons he does not yet fully understand. He feels within himself that the murder is not something which can be 'explained', and that even if it could be explained it would make little real difference where it matters—in the lives of those most directly affected by the killing, the families. The understanding of such violence is beyond the reach of the systematic and coherent knowledge of Sandy's books of philosophy. This is real, and must be faced in its nakedness, without the aid of bookish knowledge, a prominent motif throughout the novel. Words and concepts induce only false vision, and Sandy imagines that Allan has come back to the croft, but when he awakes properly he realises that it is the policeman who has come in. Yet, as Sandy knows, there is a way of knowing that is beyond the mechanical: he had instinctively shielded Allan 'beyond thought, before its grip could get him'. And it is clear that Sandy equates the usefulness of conceptual thought with the usefulness of the words on the pages of his book: it bears little relevance to the specific reality of his situation. Sandy's appeal is to a higher reason, a reason beyond conventional ideas of right and wrong, because he fully understands that all such concepts are relative:

> The conflict between right and wrong
> Is the sickness of the mind.[1]

It is this awareness that sets Sandy apart from Mr Davidson and Nicol, and gives him the possibility of greater understanding. They operate on the level of thought, on the basis of a series of formulated assumptions, in a self-perpetuating system of conventional responses to experience. In the end, this is not enough, and it is the apparently ridiculous figure of Sandy who is able to put an end to the violence which policeman and minister in their different ways prolong.

Sandy's apparent dullness of mind is an indication of the extent to which he is unable and unwilling to externalise his response to the murder in conventional terms. In this he is clearly contrasted with Nicol and with the minister. Nicol, in his increasing obsession with the hunt for Allan Innes in ways far beyond his official function as the keeper of law and order, is almost the exact opposite of Sandy.

> As Nicol replaced the glass funnel, his face seemed not only thinner but darker in a disturbing avid way. He had taken the night in with him; and then Sandy realised that it was not the dark night outside, but the dark inner world in which the fellow now lived. (p.214)

Nicol is trapped within the dark webs of his obsessive thoughts, and now lives entirely in a nightmare landscape of suspicion, and the threat of constant violence. For a man like Nicol, this had clearly been a danger all along, as Sandy had recognised.

> As they ate, Nicol had to pursue his questioning of Sandy's 'philosophy', but his manner never became warm or intimate yet it was clearly natural to him as to a man who must see how the bits and pieces make the machine. Once an idea got into his head, he could not lightly forsake it. (pp.63–4)

For Nicol, the world is a collection of bits and pieces that fit together neatly, and are easily explained. It is this easily explained world that is destroyed by the murder of his brother, an event which does not fit and which, by its very nature reveals to Nicol things within himself which do not fit either. Sandy, on the other hand, even in his troubled state of mind, is aware of life as a creative and expansive state which cannot be contained by thought; there is much that will not fit a convenient pattern, but to Sandy this knowledge is liberating: 'the mystery, that yet was no mystery in the moment of being stirred but something known in the region beyond thought, something that thought could never lay hold of . . .' (p.115) Sandy is aware of the 'warm feeling at life's real core' a feeling which is 'pure and untouched by thought', an awareness based on the knowledge that the world is something more than that which can be rationally explained by man and from this awareness he draws a quiet enduring strength. Thus time after time in *Bloodhunt*, he is seen to experience a mindless, wordless communion with the world in which he lives.

> He was in no hurry and it was going to be a good day. The clouds were small and high and gave to the sky a summer blue, the blue

133

of promise. The wind was in the west but not much of it and not cold. When he got the smell of the birches, the promise in the blue was confirmed and he stood for a little time among the slim silvered trunks. Compared with man the earth was very old, but old as it was it was quickening with a youth vivid as boyhood. He got the smell of it, the sharp acrid smell that tingled in the blood, or very nearly for his old flesh would hardly let it in. But it was there, and if he could scrape away the old flesh and the barnacles of time, he might feel the swish and surge of it. (p.240)

Expressed in the familiar imagery of the natural world, this evokes Sandy's state of mind in a way that might at first appear formulaic and repetitive. But just as the experience of Enlightenment is the same yet vastly different for each person who experiences it, so Gunn's writing has the capacity to evoke an experience in its universal and its particular aspects at one and the same time. Here, on the moor, Sandy's understanding is both specific and universal, as is seen in the way that last sentence is not simply about an old man's wishing he was younger. It is a statement that shows a clear understanding of the way that Enlightenment is achieved, not by adding something to one's life, but by clearing away the accumulation of opinions and conditioned responses in order to see simply and clearly just what is there. One of the most important realisations in the experience of Enlightenment is the recognition that life, seen with the renewed vision of Enlightenment, is no different than it was before: one is simply more aware of its significance at every point. So, in Gunn, each moment of awareness echoes and develops previous moments. The process is continual, just as the development of awareness in life is always going on, even when apparently forgotten, because it is a creative process fully in accord with the creativity which is life itself.

Such experiences as Sandy's are moments in which man is aware of life's wholeness and integrity, the very qualities which violence attacks. For violence breaks the circle of wholeness by being essentially an expression of separation from the world: it is a denial of man's place in the scheme of things, and so is ultimately self-destructive. This is why Sandy sees violence as 'the most terrible of all things, and—in the end—the most tiresome': tiresome because 'It empties life to the very dregs'. In contrast to the expansiveness of Sandy's awareness of life's creativity, violence is an attempt to restrict and contain, to keep things within man's control, to make them fit the pattern. And violence is not only physical but is also spiritual. Indeed one of the deadliest forms of violence is that of abstract thought. Professor Hart has succinctly described the importance of this in Gunn's fiction: 'Gunn's archetypal murderer is one who seeks, by intellectual disintegration, to destroy his victim spiritually.'[2]

'Thought', of course, in this context has a specific connotation. In stressing the dangers inherent in abstract thought, Gunn does not advocate living a life given over to the gratification of unbridled lust. Rather, he is concerned to highlight the futility of man's capacity for abstract thought if all that is achieved by it is the creation of more and more ideas *about* life while the actual experience of living itself is forgotten. The end result of such an approach to the world is the ludicrous spectacle of man being reduced to the level of trying to find reasons for living at all.

Krishnamurti is explicit on the dangers inherent in such an attitude. Asked about the purpose of living, during the course of a talk he answered:

> You say, 'Is this the purpose of living?'—but why do you want a purpose for living?—live. Living is its own purpose; why do you want a purpose? Look: each one has his own purpose, the religious man his purpose, the scientist his purpose, the family man his purpose and so on, all dividing. The life of a man who has a purpose is breeding violence.[3]

And earlier in the same talk he had identified the source of violence:

> The source of violence is the 'me', the ego, the self, which expresses itself in so many ways—in division, in trying to become or be somebody—which divides itself as the 'me' and the 'not me', as the unconscious and the conscious; the 'me' that identifies with the family or not with the family, with the community or not with

the community and so on. It is like a stone dropped in a lake: the waves spread and spread, at the centre is the 'me'. As long as the 'me' survives in any form, very subtly or grossly, there must be violence.[4]

Violence comes from the 'me', from the life of a man who is able to regard the world as separate from himself and who approaches it with a sense of purpose, trying to make it fit his particular idea of how things should be, with little real sense of how things actually are. Sandy, living on the edge of the community, quietly waiting for his death, has no purpose in living; his 'me', his sense of identity is fully integrated with the world around him. This is conveyed through those moments of thought-less communion with the world, moments in which he seems to merge with the very landscape, and through the way he is seen as an embodiment of the traditional wisdom of the community.

In this he is contrasted with the community's other main representative, the minister. The minister, because of his doctrinal stance, is a man apart from the community, both in his own eyes and in the eyes of the people who look to him for spiritual guidance. The contrast is highlighted by the realisation, as early as Chapter 2, that Sandy and the minister are good-humoured rivals of long-standing. Mr Davidson advocates a specifically Christian approach to living, while Sandy, as an old pagan, shies away from questions of doctrine and dogma, finding the more pragmatic traditional ways more congenial. And this debate is central to the novel's meaning: it is the ancient debate between love and duty. 'The manger and the hay and life's new cry; beyond it, that hunt. Of all the stories man had made only two were immortal: the story of Cain and the story of Christ.' (p.233) Love is irrational, beyond explanation by conscious thought, and cannot be contained, therefore it is a state of freedom. Duty, on the other hand, involves living in accordance with a particular code of behaviour devised with a particular result in mind. Inevitably it leads to violence because it induces division in man and between men. Love, being spontaneous, does not conform to any pattern and is infinitely flexible and so able to defuse violence.

When Sandy returns some stolen money to the minister, knowing that Allan's younger brother had taken it in the hope of getting it to Allan, he pleads for the minister to exercise Christ's creed of love and forgiveness. And on this occasion he succeeds. Later, however, the different attitudes of the two men are focussed in a discussion of the violent sensationalism of many aspects of modern culture. Mr Davidson tells Sandy he is disappointed in him:

> 'You treat the matter without the deep consideration it demands, my friend . . . If they must have violence and blood and brutality, I said to them, if they must have fear in their picture houses to curdle their blood with satisfaction, then, I said, give them the fear of God.'
> Sandy nodded. 'Either that or the love of Christ.' (pp.190–1)

And yet, through their conversation the minister seems to embrace Sandy's position more and more. He is moved not by abstract arguments, but by the example of Sandy's nature.

> 'More than once you have said what has remained with myself, and, perhaps, in the silent watches—I hope I may do more than forgive you for your reference to the love of Christ, over-ready as it was. My fight is often a solitary one, and sometimes I have wondered if I have been moved more by the fight than the substance.'
> 'Never,' said Sandy. 'No, no. Someone must see man's duty and be prepared to act. I wish I had your strength and your firmness.'
> He spoke with such sad sincerity that the minister was moved . . . The minister poured two small drops, more by way of token or communion than anything else . . .
> 'I bring you this new commandment,' said the minister, and paused, as though somehow words that Sandy had dropped so lightly stole now upon him unawares and troubled him. There was a short silent travail of the spirit, then humbly, yet not too humbly, the minister repeated the most revolutionary saying the world had yet heard: 'I bring you this new commandment: love one another.' (pp.192–3)

Sandy has no 'purpose' in his life, no dogma or principles to uphold, so he is able to encounter life freely. It is this inner

freedom that communicates itself to the minister and helps him
to a greater awareness of what is actually happening. It is a
freedom that comes from his avoidance of a strict sense of
identity, of the 'me' which Krishnamurti isolates as the root of
violence.

One of the major structural devices of the book reveals a link
between the murderer, Allan Innes, injured and hiding out on
an island in a loch, and his protector Sandy, confined to his
croft by an injury incurred when taking his cow to the bull. The
minister draws attention to the link by remarking that Sandy's
injury is a result of the sexual impulse, 'the outward manifestation of the inward riot'. As the minister continues it is clear that
this violent incident is linked to the murder of Robert Nicol in a
quarrel over a girl. Unlike Sandy, 'Sex and blood and brutality'
is all the minister can see in the modern world. But the link
between Allan and Sandy had been clear much earlier. Sandy
had known Allan well, and feels for the boy alone on the moor.
His own injury is a symbol of that link between boy and man,
youth and age. The doctor had prescribed sleeping pills for
Sandy so that he is able to enjoy a good night's sleep, which
contrasts sharply with the plight of Allan.

> When he awoke finally in the morning Sandy was conscious of
> having had a wonderful sleep. Twice during the night he had
> come to himself, but hazily and knowing that sleep was waiting
> for him. Extraordinary what two little pills could do . . .
> Sandy luxuriated in the weakness of having given in to drugs,
> then he stirred and the calm was broken. Stoically he tried to
> move his body and from the sharp pains a flush mounted. When
> he wiped his forehead he found it cold and damp and as he
> brought his right hand down it shook . . .
> [Allan] would have had a bad night on the Crannock.
> Everything sodden and not a spark of fire. To lie down would be
> impossible—and fatal if he tried. He would have to keep on the
> move. But he couldn't move much in the dark, and it would have
> been pitch black under the low skies and rain last night. (p.125)

The passage moves from Sandy's feeling of comfort and well-
being to a consciousness of his own pain as he tries to move and
from there, through images of pain, coldness and dampness, to

a vivid identification with Allan Innes on the Crannock. The link between Sandy and Allan is further established by the use of an image which Gunn had used in *Highland River* to symbolise the link between Kenn and the salmon. When Kenn, nine years old and exhausted by the struggle with the great fish, finally takes the salmon he lays it on the riverbank and falls beside it to rest and regain his breath. In *Bloodhunt*, after Sandy has with great difficulty recovered Allan's body from the peat bog, he is completely drained, and stretches himself beside the dead boy to recover. And it is in Gaelic that Sandy addresses Allan's body for the community's new language has not yet acquired the depth of feeling which will allow it to be used in moments of extreme emotion. 'The body turned over and came down against his knees. The thin face was smeared with soft black peat. The eyes were wide open. He felt the forehead. In a quiet anguished voice he said, "Allan, *mo laochain*".' (p.245) The words 'my hero' do not convey much intellectually, but emotionally they encompass all the wisdom and love of the community of which both men are representatives.

The transparency of Sandy's character, the lack of a consistent 'me' by which others can claim to know him, allows the reader to see him not so much as a conventional literary character, but rather as the essence of the community. It is the minister's recognition of Sandy's essential nature that leads him to reconsider his own ethical stance, and contact with Sandy is almost too much for Liz Murison in her distraught and anxious state.

> Sandy had a way of speaking quietly, kindly, that went very near the bone. Again all her movements stopped, her head went down, as if someone were saying grace at table. Then her shoulders heaved and he heard the draw of breath in her nostrils. She did her best, she trembled, her features became contorted above her pressed lips, but the sob broke through . . .
>
> It was the last thing she meant to do, poor girl. She would have wanted to be cool and capable. Sandy had a profound intuition of the pitiful nature of the human condition. (p.146)

Sandy's voice is not just a man's voice; it is the voice of a whole culture, distilled to its purest essence. Elsewhere in Gunn this is symbolised by Gaelic song. Here it is carried in the quietness of an old man's voice, a quietness born of wisdom and under-standing, and based on the awareness of the mystery that lies at the heart of life.

As an old man Sandy's thoughts often turn to that final mystery, death. Indeed his whole life as a crofter, on the periphery of his community, might be seen as a waiting for death. This is not a morbid attitude, however, but one based on an acceptance of life's inevitable changes. On a walk near his croft Sandy had experienced a great revelation about the nature of death so that the thought of it no longer troubles him.

> The sun and the air, the roll of the hills, the ups and downs, perhaps brought back something of the sea. Anyway, he could hardly have enough of it, and when at last he saw his croft in the distance he sat down, reluctant to end his day, to lose this happiness, with the sun and the wind warming and blowing past him, knitting him into them and into everything with a sense of well-being throughout his utterly tired body that was rare beyond telling.
>
> And then, as simply as a thought might come to him when taking his porridge, he saw that to pass out of his body was in the order of things, now revealed; not an end and not quite a translation, but precisely a passing on and away. At that moment it would have been easy and pleasant to die. He could have gone.
>
> Not only had death no sting, *it did not matter*. (pp.57–8)

And Sandy's 'philosophy', his understanding of 'the order of things' is made apparent to the reader not as a set of abstract concepts, but as an attitude of creative openness before life. He has thought long and hard on various things and has realised that there can be no conclusions: words and abstract concepts are not enough when faced by life in its swift-moving reality.

Much of Sandy's story in *Bloodhunt* concerns the way in which he is startled out of his complacency by the whole business of the murder and the manhunt into an examination of his own basic attitudes to life. He is sickened by the outbreak of violence, because in his own life he has been trying to get beyond it, trying to live in a way of non-violence. But, however undesirable it may be, violence *is* present in man. Ignoring it will not lessen its impact. Indeed, refusal to acknowledge man's potential for violence and destruction only heightens its effect when it does break out. If violence is to be transcended, then man must acknowledge and strive to comprehend this aspect of his nature. Only then does he have the possibility of being able to live more creatively. Sandy himself is continually fighting against the desire for any easy peace of mind, the desire to forget about it all: knowing that he himself at least is safe. But in the end he is unable to give in to the temptation.

> I'm taking care of myself, he thought, as he sat down in his own chair. I am not going to be involved.
> There was something pitiful in that. There was indeed. The thin bubble that was man's own self, nursing itself to the end, sheltering itself still from the near burst.
> But that wasn't quite the whole of it. Not quite. (p.50)

It is not quite the whole of it because Sandy is able to see his selfishness for what it is, and is able to put fear aside and act with compassion. Such an attitude is based on a deep understanding of the way in which life continually eludes man's attempts to categorise it. Sandy knows full well that the drama in which he is involved is no simple battle between good and evil, right and wrong, but is a more complex situation which involves facing up to the fact that there is much in life which cannot be explained by these categories and can only be approached by a continually evolving responsiveness to concrete situations as they arise. It is an attitude based on an awareness of the void which underlies all human experience. 'Mystery. That was the last word, the word you came to at the end. No corner of its coverlet could you lift. Man's stoicism was not a creed, only his last attitude. He went without finding out. He went into the darkness.' (pp.180–1) For Sandy the whole world is 'potent with mystery beyond the mind's grasp' and life is a continual facing up to the implications of this mystery. It is there in the whole business of the murder and the ensuing manhunt, but it confronts him most starkly when he finds Allan's body on the moor near the end, when his own personal feelings are most directly involved. 'He spoke to Allan several

141

times, for the waste of young life troubled Sandy and he could see little meaning or purpose in it. It would have been more like the thing if he himself had been lying in Allan's place. But the mystery did not work out that way and all thought or sentiment about it was vanity and folly.' (p.246)

Sandy's life of solitary contemplation has expanded his knowledge and awareness of this 'country of the spirit' and has given him the strength to carry on when, to the conscious mind at least, all seems vanity and folly. This other landscape of spiritual experience is a realm where conceptual thought is useless, as it upholds the illusion of man's separation from his environment and so obscures clear vision. Once the desire to think consciously in this region is transcended, then man begins to *see*. This ability to *see* the world in its 'suchness' is the clear vision of meditation. Sandy's contemplative lifestyle has given him a clear intimation of this, in a way which yet retains its essential mystery. 'All this loomed before him in the region beyond thought, beyond words. It was the region he had slowly been drawing nearer to, but now it was obscure, with enigmas like rocks, and an air above it like a dim light.' (p.166)

That this is not simply some obscure metaphysical quirk of an old man's imagination is implicit in Sandy's symbolic function as the embodiment of the values of a whole community. It is here that the book's claims to universality lie; Sandy is at once an old man, by turns ridiculous and profound, and a symbol of the essential values of the traditional community. The connection is made explicitly in Chapter 14.

> [Liz Murison] had come because she would have heard stories about him from the lads in past years, how he lived beyond the edge of the ordinary world, in that region into which they escaped and found life, and made, no doubt, wild stories about it, full of laughter. (p.149)

Sandy's capacity to see directly into the nature of things has grown out of his close observation of the landscape and the people among whom he lives. It is a capacity which is important both in his dealings with individuals and in his attitude to the world at large. He is highly perceptive as to the nature of his relationships with others. Shortly after Liz has come to his croft, Sandy has a clear vision of her emotional state. 'She was dumb, but dumb in the region of feeling, beyond thought, and this he understood and it affected him.' (p.144) Where others see only stupidity and obstinacy, Sandy is able to grasp the reasons for Liz giving this impression of herself, and this compassionate attitude extends beyond the particular to see the universal aspects of Liz's situation.

These moments of insight are consistently represented as 'visions' whether as dreams, vivid pictorial images, or even with the suggestion of second sight; 'his vision passed between times and places like a flying bird'. Wakened from sleep by the crying of Liz Murison's child, Sandy is back in his own childhood, the barriers of space and time transcended by the quality of vision.

> Two or three hours later, Sandy, startled out of sleep, heard the thin puling of a child and the low voices of two women. At once he was a small boy again listening to those very sounds. The illusion was so remarkably strong that he dwelt in it, even while the real situation seeped into its edges. It had all happened before. He saw his mother with a vivid clarity, nursing her last child in its fatal illness, his father's quiet weather-burnt face, his brothers and two sisters, all older than he. The warmth of their lives, the look in their eyes, the old croft house—the whole came about him, almost tangibly; he breathed its air, his young heart caught its beat, his eyes saw every characteristic movement. They were there solidly yet not solidly but fluidly like water, and yet not like water but illusively like air, essential presences painted on a timeless air. (pp.230–1)

The whole piece moves in an attempt to evoke the elusiveness of these 'essential presences', and Sandy's power of vision is a symbol of spiritual insight and awareness.

It is with this same quality of vision that Sandy sees the end of Nicol's blood-hunt. Although he does not actually see how Allan Innes dies, he follows the movements of Allan and Nicol on the moor through his telescope, and witnesses their final confrontation. It is a hunt he has seen also in his own mind, with 'the awful compelling power of second sight':

143

. . . now and then he caught a glimpse of Nicol's face, his sharp searching features vanishing into a landscape, towards the shores of Loch Deoch, with the Crannock lying off the upper end.

And he saw Allan's face, its scrubby pallor, its hunted criminal look, the hacking cough.

As in lenses that opened and shut these two figures came and went over glimpses of country . . . (p.172)

The moor, as in *Highland River*, is symbolic as well as actual. A network of imagery connects the moor with darkness and violence throughout the novel, and its wild, broken country is the stage upon which these forces work themselves out. The moor is a desolation of the spirit, 'primeval and barren', and yet to Sandy's clear vision the moor has another aspect and is a symbol of profound wisdom, a wisdom beyond words which apprehends life directly in its infinite beauty and variety.

Nicol's killing of Allan Innes on that moor, and Sandy's response to the killing, represent the eternal struggle between wisdom and knowledge, love and duty, and shows how wisdom and love always prevail. This is not because they are superior philosophies, but rather because in eschewing the easy answers of a philosophy they allow man to face reality directly. If man is then able to comprehend the workings of that reality then he is immediately involved in the natural, creative, Way of life itself. Once this happens then his whole attitude to the world is changed, and understanding not judgement is seen as the most relevant virtue.[5]

Yet the adoption of this new attitude is no easy course to take, as is seen in Sandy's response to the killing. Knowing that he is the only witness to Nicol's hounding of Allan Innes to his death, he is faced with the choice of performing his public duty and reporting the matter to the proper authorities, a course which would lead to legal proceedings ending in a hanging or a prison sentence for Nicol, or of accepting that the violence has now exhausted itself and refusing to stir it up again. After some deliberation his instinct tells him to take the latter course, just as he had earlier shielded Allan from the duty-bound policeman. This, however, is not to condone violence or to evade one's responsibilities. Rather, it reveals an understanding of the

144

nature of violence and how it is present in all of us. Sandy's understanding is based not just on the solitary contemplation of his later years, but is solidly based on some personal experience deep in his past as a young sailor in a foreign country, and the death of the girl, Maria, who had helped him. With such an understanding of the nature of violence, Sandy is beyond the futility of judging, of apportioning blame to Allan or Nicol, or to both.

> What might happen to Nicol came as ashes into Sandy's mouth. In all conscience, there had been enough violence and his mind called halt. He felt like an old man of the tribe, as the tribe had been and might be again, with decision in his hands for the living, and the responsibility for that decision . . .
> After a little while he got up and went slowly on. Right and wrong. Ay, that was easy. But the new commandment: love one another . . . (pp.248–9)

And despite his own doubts and apprehensiveness, the action of the novel has shown Sandy's response to the violence to be ultimately more enlightened than that of those who, like the minister, have a measuring rod handy by which they can judge human actions. Sandy's more comprehensive vision includes within it an acknowledgement of the existence of much that is illogical or inexplicable in human behaviour. Violence is but one aspect of this, and by refusing to indulge in the vanity of thinking that he has all the answers, Sandy is able to perceive life in its creative movement, a movement that is inexplicable in the terms of logic alone.

> There was a knowledge beyond reason. It was not to be looked at, questions had no meaning. Things happened.
> Human beings moved from one place to another, one day to another. They went on doing this, beyond creeds and massacres, desperation and death.
> So long as life was left, it moved. That was about as far as thought could go. He saw patterns of the movement, figures walking on blind feet. (pp.152–3)

The movement of life is beyond the grasp of the conscious mind, and violence begins with the attempt to 'freeze' the movement and formalise the patterns. In his refusal to do this, and in his compassionate response to everyone involved in the violence of *Bloodhunt*, Sandy is the living guardian of the values of life and delight, values which are crucial to man's survival. *Bloodhunt* is no simple account of a murder in a backwater of the Highlands, but is a book which confronts the nature of violence and is able to suggest a positive response to it.

SEEKING THE MASTER
The Other Landscape 1954

The wisdom attained by Sandy in *Bloodhunt* is based on his understanding of life as an endless process of creation and destruction, 'potent with mystery beyond the mind's grasp'. It is significant that Sandy is an old man because this is the wisdom of age, learned over a lifetime of trial and error. For others, however, there might be a chance of being guided along the Way by a master, by someone who has gone that way before and is able to keep one on the right track. Gunn's last novel, *The Other Landscape* (1954), describes one man's encounter with such a person, and is a record of his attempts to understand him. It is not one of his best books. There is much in it that is simply asserted by the author, rather than worked out in the interaction of characters and plot and so made real to the reader. But it is an immensely interesting book for those readers who have followed the deepening of Gunn's understanding of the world of the spirit.

Recounted in the first person, *The Other Landscape* tells of Walter Urquhart's encounter with Douglas Menzies, an artist living in a remote Highland community. Urquhart seeks out the author of a typescript sent to an editor friend of his and after tracing it to Menzies finds him living in a white house on the cliffs. The local people regard him as mentally unstable following the death of his wife Annabel in tragic circumstances. Such a bald summary, however, gives no real indication of the real subject of the novel.

The Other Landscape is about the possibility of spiritual

awakening, an awakening that can only come about through the adoption of a particular attitude of mind, an attitude of receptivity and passivity, the realisation of the meditative mind.

> I sat on the beach for a while. Here a bit of old iron stuck out of the shingle, there a rib from a buried keel. The sea water brimmed with a soft hiss. One listens as naturally as the seas brims, listens *back*. I realised I hadn't done this for a long time.
>
> One can see mute things with an extraordinary clarity. Then a touch, just a touch, of clairvoyance seems to come out of the listening and the mind grows abnormally sensitive. The slow movement of the water, its mounting rhythm, the crash, the recession . . . (p.32)

The mind's sensitivity to such moments of insight is increased by an encounter with one who is further along the 'Way', and who is thus able to adopt the role of master. In *The Other Landscape*, Douglas Menzies is clearly such a man. His conversations with Urquhart are reverberant with hidden meaning, something more often sensed than really understood by the younger man. Yet even this is enough to nudge Urquhart nearer to Enlightenment. 'As we sparred away . . . he came alive, and I got that sensation again, as always in his presence, of space about to open up, and whether the space was outward or inward the expansive effect was the same.' (pp.300–1)

This ability to develop receptivity in others, to open up our limited perception, is the mark of the master. Indefinable by nature, it is a quality that is capable of infinite expression, and which once seen is immediately recognised. Professor Suzuki, in a little-known autobiographical essay, describes clearly his perception of this quality in his own master, Kosen.

> One interview with him impressed me particularly. He was having breakfast on a veranda overlooking a pond, sitting at a table on a rather rough little chair and eating rice gruel which he kept ladling out of an earthenware pot into his bowl. After I had made my three bows to him he told me to sit opposite him on another chair. I remember nothing that was said at that time, but every movement he made—the way he motioned me to sit on the chair, and the way he helped himself to the rice gruel from the pot—struck me with great force. Yes, that is exactly the way a Zen

monk must behave, I thought. Everything about him had a directness and simplicity and sincerity and, of course, something more which cannot be specifically described.[1]

This is the calmer aspect of the master's self-possession and internal strength, but Zen literature abounds in stories of its more dynamic expression, and it is not for nothing that a meeting with a master is approached with some measure of trepidation:

> . . . the masters had no qualms if they thought it necessary to shake the pupils roughly. Rinzai for one was noted for the directness and incisiveness of his dealings; the point of his sword cut through the heart of the opponent. The monk Jo (Ting) was one of his disciples, and when he asked the master what the fundamental principle of Buddhism was, Rinzai came down from his straw chair, and taking hold of the monk slapped him with the palm of his hand, and let him go. Jo stood still without knowing what to make of the whole procedure, when a by-standing monk blamed him for not bowing to the master. While doing so, Jo all of a sudden awoke to the truth of Zen.[2]

It was encounters such as these that became formalised into the *koan* system and the *sanzen* interview between master and student in which the student has to present an answer to his own particular *koan*. Even in present-day Zen monasteries this interview with the master is a daunting event for the serious student.

> To a young Zen monk the *roshi* . . . stands as a symbol of the utmost patriarchal authority, and he usually plays the role to perfection—being normally a man advanced in years, fierce and 'tigerish' in aspect, and, when formally robed and seated for the *sanzen* interview, a person of supreme presence and dignity. In this role he constitutes a living symbol of everything that makes one afraid of being spontaneous, everything that prompts the most painful and awkward self-consciousness. He assumes this role as an *upāya*, a skilful device, for challenging the student to find enough 'nerve' to be perfectly natural in the presence of this formidable archetype.[3]

Both the formal *sanzen* interview and the more informal encounters are teaching situations in which knowledge is passed on from master to student. It may be that the student is not yet ready to receive this knowledge, in which case it is necessary that the master repeat the lesson until such time as he is capable of receiving it. What is taught, what is learned, through such encounters is a new way of relating to the world. The effort required of the student to understand what the master is revealing to him ensures that his mind is receptive to the master's teaching. Not that this teaching is an intellectual matter of the mind alone.

> The whole emphasis of [Zen] discipline is placed on the intuitive grasping of the inner truth deeply hidden in our consciousness. And this truth thus revealed or awakened within oneself defies intellectual manipulation, or at least cannot be imparted to others through any dialectical formulas. It must come out of oneself, grow within oneself, and become one with one's own being. What others, that is, ideas or images, can do, is to indicate the way where lies the truth. This is what Zen masters do.[4]

At first glance all this might seem a long way from the world of Gunn's novels, but on closer inspection it is clear that neither the idea of a spiritual master, nor the transmission of such a person's knowledge is new in Gunn. As early as *Sun Circle* and *Butcher's Broom*, with the character of Dark Mairi and of course the Master himself, Gunn had shown himself keenly aware of the existence of such people. And as the case of Mairi makes abundantly clear there is here nothing esoteric or mysterious, only an absolute practicality that knows always when and how to act for the best result: 'Where all is magic, only the utterly practical person like Mairi can use it, troubled neither by the self-consciousness of the sceptic nor the idealism of the poet.'[5] This is clear also from other master/pupil relationships in Gunn such as that of Art and Hector in *Young Art and Old Hector* and *The Green Isle of the Great Deep*, a relationship so realistically observed as part of the Highland scene, yet with myriad possibilities of interpretation. What Art learns from Hector is often something so specific as to have meaning for Art alone. This is as it should be. Each man has to live his own life, make his own discovery of its meaning. But beyond the specifics what he learns is the new way of relating to the world that is the teaching of the Zen masters. Again there is no mystery here. Mystery only confuses, while the aim and method of Zen requires directness and simplicity.

> Drinking tea, eating rice,
> I pass my time as it comes;
> Looking down at the stream, looking up at the mountains,
> How serene and relaxed I feel indeed![6]

But this clarity and simplicity is not achieved easily. It is no accident that it is Gunn's more elderly characters who reveal this quality most strongly, for this is a wisdom matured out of experience. The same pattern is revealed in *The Other Landscape*, with Menzies, the older, more experienced man in a position to pass on some of his knowledge to the younger man. But although Menzies appears to Urquhart as master of the inner regions he is exploring, it is clear to the reader that he is in fact still engaged in the quest, still actively seeking the Way which Urquhart imagines him to have found.

Such wisdom is not passed on conventionally. Rather, it is revealed in hints and suggestions which emerge from between the lines of the master's words. The ability to recognise these pointers for what they are comes from the pupil's ability to develop a particular empathy with the master; a state of mind that responds not to the ideas and concepts the master may put forward, but responds directly to the master's demonstration of the nature of Enlightenment in his own person. Traditionally it is believed that Zen began with this realisation that however much can be taught philosophically, there is something more that forever evades the grasp of conceptual thought.

> The legendary story of the origin of Zen in India runs as follows: Sakyamuni was once engaged at the Mount of the Holy Vulture in preaching to a congregation of his disciples. He did not resort to any lengthy verbal discourse to explain his point, but simply lifted a bouquet of flowers before the assemblage, which was presented to him by one of his lay-disciples. Not a word came out of his mouth. Nobody understood the meaning of this except the old venerable Mahakasyapa, who quietly smiled at the master, as if he fully comprehended the purport of this silent but eloquent teaching on the part of the Enlightened One.[7]

151

But this transmission of knowledge can only take place if the recipient is sufficiently prepared to recognise the truth that is presented to him. In the case of the Zen student this state of readiness is achieved through work with *zāzen* and the *koan*. For Walter Urquhart, in *The Other Landscape*, it is the development of his work as an anthropologist.

> In a way I laid myself open for it; yet to do so was natural enough to a man in my profession, who has to make sure that traditional modes of behaviour or response are not confused with so-called fundamental truths about human nature. A job has to be tackled objectively and the facts recorded as clearly and inclusively as possible so that others, working outside the field, may make assessments or reach conclusions, like psychologists or even psychiatrists. (p.46)

More immediately, however, it is Urquhart's reading of Menzies' typescript which has made him aware of the man's compelling power. Menzies' story, of a storm at sea, and of a love that goes beyond death, was for Urquhart a first glimpse of the 'other' landscape, of a world beyond man's conscious control. 'Cliffs and storms and the almighty Wrecker . . . it also had an extraordinary intimacy between a man and a woman that was more than disturbing, almost unbearable, because it was carried beyond the personal.' (p.12) The story opens Urquhart's mind to the mystery of this region beyond the personal, and makes him conscious of his own ignorance of it. From then onwards he is in a state of mind conducive to learning: 'Knowledge of ignorance is the end of so much knowledge and the beginning of wisdom'.[8] All he lacks is a teacher.

It is his conviction that Menzies can fulfil this role that makes Urquhart so keen to seek him out: the business matter regarding the possible publication of the typescript is only an excuse. But even before he meets Menzies, his journey brings him into contact with another remarkable man, also older and more experienced, and who also it seems might be able to teach him something. This is the Major, a retired diplomat who is a resident in Urquhart's hotel. Conversation with this man makes Urquhart painfully aware of his own inexperience: 'I might have acquired some knowledge, some human facts here and there, but that was a long way from understanding, from the experience that had gone beneath the surface and endured what was encountered there.' (p.20) But Urquhart can never learn from the Major for, though the Major is a man of insight, he is quite prepared to amuse himself by using his insight to manipulate others. The Major's character offers no possibility of expanded awareness, because he is unable to go beyond the level of self-gratification. On the other hand Menzies, who is an artist, is capable of going beyond this, and so is able to pass on something of his own insight to others. The Major himself is tragically aware of this:

> . . . as the talk went on I got a quite vivid impression of what was troubling him at the deep level: he was jealous of Menzies. He knew that Menzies was the only one who could stand beside him at his utmost reach—and then go beyond. This particularly exasperated the Major because he had assured himself that there was no beyond. (p.293)

For Menzies this 'beyond' is the region in which he now lives: 'he had a unique appreciation of other modes of being. Many of us have intuitive glimpses. This man could get the whole field, the integral intuition. He could wander about in it.' (p.238) Even so, Urquhart is in no hurry to meet Menzies and tries to put off the encounter for as long as he can.

> I wasn't ready, I felt; and because it becomes a habit to attempt to rationalise any feeling, I searched about until I found a satisfactory reason, namely, that when I did meet him I must have his script with me and talk in a simple businesslike way. It was something in the writing that made me hesitate, with a sense of fear going deep, like the cliff-face. (p.10)

When they do meet for the first time it is at Menzies' run-down white house on the cliffs, and as if to lend credence to the local rumour that he has been driven insane by his wife's death, Menzies appears in the guise of a wild man accompanied by his dog:

> . . . a tawny collie with the shoulders, the head, of a development beyond the wolf . . . The hair seemed to stand up on his shoulders. He was lean but powerful. He would hunt for his food;

153

reverting to the wild. I would no more have thought of patting him than of putting my hand in a trap. (p.66)

The description of Menzies himself, the artist who has 'reverted to the wild', links him indissolubly with this dog.

As his hand screwed up the wicks the fingers straightened out from the knuckles in fine bone. These fingers would take a relentless grip . . . a chin rather pointed, as if the underlying bone in the man would not be denied . . . The skin was not ashen at all, it was drained of colour as if it had been washed incredibly clean . . . He was about my own height, five feet ten, spare, but again, with bone that showed at the shoulder ends; not the cerebral or cerebrotonic type; slim and smooth, but bony and strong or, rather, enduring, like the old hunting men. (p.62)

This daunting character is the man Urquhart acknowledges as his spiritual 'master', and from the time of this first meeting (if not indeed from the moment he had first read Menzies' typescript) Urquhart puts himself in a position to learn from Menzies. But this learning process is fraught with difficulties as Menzies, in keeping with his role as master, places many obstacles in Urquhart's path. And beyond this, even, there is the suggestion that Menzies himself has not quite mastered everything, that he also is still learning, so that for Urquhart there is no real guarantee that Menzies can teach him anything. In the region of the spirit there can be no guarantee. To ask for one betrays one's lack of faith, and reveals one's unreadiness for the quest. There is of course still doubt, but that can be used as a spur and the struggle with one's own doubts is one of the most crucial stages in the development of self-knowledge and awareness.

This learning process is brought alive to the reader through the conversations between Urquhart and Menzies which constitute the real action of the book. In Urquhart's descriptions of the conversations as they took place, and in his subsequent meditation on their significance we see the same mixture of puzzlement and belated understanding which characterises the Zen student's perception of the master: unable to take in the reality of the master immediately, he has slowly to piece

154

together his partial glimpses of the master's wholeness in the hope that next time he will be able to recognise and respond to this quality with a wholeness of his own. It may take many meetings with the master before this happens. In *The Other Landscape*, Urquhart is allowed only three extended meetings with Menzies. Yet even in three meetings there is much to learn.

But what Urquhart learns from Menzies is no codifiable 'philosophy'. Nothing is taught that can be externalised. Rather Urquhart is awakened, through contact with Menzies, to his own potential. Like Dark Mairi in *Butcher's Broom* or the Master in *Sun Circle*, Menzies is there as an *image* of a spiritual state to which we may aspire. His words also are part of this image leading always to an awareness of the essential emptiness of verbal concepts. Such an awareness is highly valued in the East. 'The word is used to convey ideas. When the ideas are apprehended, let us forget the words. How delightful to be able to talk with such a man, who has forgotten the words!'[9] Douglas Menzies is a man who has 'forgotten' the words. He constantly points out in these conversations that language, being rational, cannot penetrate the irrational, the other landscape of delight. Urquhart is quick to see the truth of this, although full understanding will only come later.

> From this sort of talk I got two quite vivid impressions: the first, that the words were so many noises about something that might be unveiled; the second, that the recurrence of the same tragic theme from its first treatment in his music to Annabel's death on that night of storm was so remarkable, so strangely startling, that a word like coincidence had no relevance and a word like recurrence was as yet only a sound to hold on to. (p.99)

Menzies' words, like those of a Zen master, are not to be understood literally as expressing ideas but rather as pointers to a region of inner spiritual experience. To Urquhart, Menzies is an example of another way of knowing, a way of knowing which has gone beyond the need to conceptualise. This other way of knowing is Enlightenment itself, and is concerned not with knowing *about* something, but with knowing it directly. 'It requires the discovery by oneself of the unreality, the relativity of all verbal assertions, concepts and ideas, including the concept of one's own "ego".'[10]

The conversations with Menzies are not intended to be philosophical 'debates': 'behind the words another silent conversation must have been going on, "the other conversation", that for each is the important one.' (p.68) This other conversation is the unspoken dialogue between teacher and taught that is the transmission of awareness. And if that sounds too grand, or too 'mystical' it should he remembered that Gunn's ability to convey accurately and convincingly the unspoken nuances of thought and feeling which lie deeply embedded in the apparent brusqueness and insensitivity of much Scottish speech is one of the marks of his greatness. And the ability to convey the meaning behind the words was a personal characteristic of Gunn himself.

> Many people have remarked that after spending an hour or two in his company, they felt elated, uplifted; the best in themselves had been brought out. There was nothing flamboyant in his personality; he was essentially a quiet, reflective man (indeed in later years something of a mystic), many of whose silences were more eloquent than speech—a characteristic reflected in the novels where much of what happens happens below the surface and emerges in a glance, an imperceptible movement, a nuance.[11]

For Walter Urquhart, Menzies is more of an enigma. From his first meeting with him he is aware of a peculiar affinity between himself and this 'wild' man. A remark by Urquhart on an author's rights provokes a satirical reply from the author himself, but Urquhart senses something else behind and beyond the satire: 'The satire may have been blasting but the artist in him savoured the word, and this affected me with an inexplicable familiarity, as though I might be tipped over into his stark region as any time.' (p.61) But this feeling of an affinity with Menzies does not make him any more approachable, and Urquhart's descriptions of his conversations with Menzies are largely the records of his own confusion, his own stumbling attempts to understand him, a recognition of the gulf that separates them. 'Whatever I would say would be on the wrong level. Commonplaces for him had got burned up. We couldn't meet.' (p.63) This realisation does nothing to put Urquhart at his ease. Menzies knows this and plays on the younger man's uncertainty, not even answering questions.

> He didn't even answer. He stood watching me, the measuring satire quite undisguised. The lips were slightly parted but straight, drawn thin. There was a movement at the corner of the left eye, a flickering. If I got up and went off now I would be conscious of having behaved in a way so indescribably trivial that I should never be able to recall it without a knot in the flesh. (p.63)

Like the Zen master in the *sanzen* interview Menzies deliberately heightens Urquhart's self-consciousness: 'His directness could turn my mind into a blank'. The result of this is to make Urquhart cripplingly aware of the gap between his ego and his 'second self'. Until one is fully aware of the extent of that gap then there can be no hope of reconciliation. Menzies' tactic of intensifying Urquhart's self-consciousness is a means of making him more aware of this, and of showing him that if he continues to regard the master in this way, as another ego, then he will learn nothing. He must go beyond the personal, must learn to see the essential Menzies.

In his efforts to drive Urquhart beyond the personal, Menzies, for all his silences, is not against verbal discussion, and as Urquhart soon realises, 'this man would use talk like a weapon'. This is most apparent in the way in which he delights in exposing Urquhart's habit of talking in clichés. Struggling to explain what he had found striking in Menzies' writing, Urquhart is forced to accept the cliché Menzies offers him to finish his sentence, and so acknowledge the clichéd nature of his whole speech. 'Let's have some more of your clichés', Menzies goads him, and when Urquhart's next attempt to say something about the writing lapses into banality Menzies is again only too pleased to supply the appropriate cliché.

> 'The reader feels that the writer has experienced with an intense clarity of vision what he, the reader, can see only as—as—'
> 'As in a glass darkly'. (p.65)

This time, however, Urquhart is prepared to carry the fight to Menzies by giving an added twist to the expression.

> I looked straight at him. 'Yes,' I said. I held his eyes and added,
> 'The degree of darkness being in inverse ratio to the intuitive
> insight.' (p.65)

Menzies appreciates the gesture, and Urquhart begins to feel he
is gradually being accepted, gradually beginning to understand
the man.

> That did something to him. Anyway, it cleared his face. Possibly I
> knew then what my words meant. I was dead solemn, too, and
> very pointed. The humour of it got him in a way that made of his
> smile almost a silent laugh as he swung off the chair and from that
> obscure corner, which he had considered twice already, picked up
> a small tin milk-pail by its wire handle. The bright tin winked in
> the direct light; it would hold two to three pints of milk. Twice the
> fellow had denied his instinct to be hospitable. Now he was going
> to give me a glass of Mrs Maclellan's milk. (p.65)

But it is not milk that Menzies pours. It is rum, and from this
sharing of spirits the relationship between the two men
changes. Urquhart begins to 'connect' more with Menzies,
begins to lose some of his self-consciousness and respond to
Menzies on his own level.

But Menzies is ever in control, and while Urquhart sits
'witless', he himself talks about his writing, emphasising the
futility of attempting to understand it in the categories of
literary criticism, again trying to force Urquhart to respond on a
level beyond the personal:

> '. . . the theme suffered a sea change into music as an art where
> the actors are the implications of the themes, reforming and
> shaping them as though they were so many myths or symbols that
> come and go, as such things do come and go in that region of
> shadows to which you may penetrate—if you must, and can keep
> your head. In that region you will take your old notions with you
> and expect to be able to answer your own questions in their terms.
> At first: what is the symbol of a wrecker? Then: what is the
> wrecker a symbol of? And so on until you are bogged in futility—
> and begin to realise that your old notions don't apply.' (p.98)

Bogged in futility himself, Urquhart begins to recognise and
respond to the ease with which Menzies is able to control the

situation. 'He went on in this inexorable way, never wildly, but with an abnormal penetration. And then I realised that he was hunting *me* out as well. He knew what was going on inside my mind. He had become an expert hunter of the inner region.' (p.71) By this time Urquhart has rejected the local rumour that Menzies is mentally unhinged and he is quite prepared to see that he is simply operating on a different level. His mastery of this way of living is obvious to the younger man who recognises it as something to which he must aspire himself.

But this is no easy task. It is difficult enough in itself but it is further complicated by the unpredictability of Menzies who is himself engaged on a quest into the unknown, a confrontation with the destructive aspect of God, the Wrecker. This is a direct result of the tragic death of his wife, Annabel. That had been the shock that had woken Menzies up to the absolute nature of the 'other' landscape. Something in Menzies is unable to accept Annabel's death: it is too near, too personal, to be transcended and this has caused his true nature to be distorted. Not until he is able to face the fact of Annabel's death will Menzies be free. Urquhart realises this quite early in his dealings with Menzies and all the time they are speaking Annabel is never far away. All their convoluted talk about reality and illusion is really talk about death and immortality.

> 'Only these two words have become conventional dead stops. They pull down the blinds.' With the help of the rum, he had certainly worked me up.
> Then I saw that he was smiling and I realised that I had at last quite naturally spoken of death and after-death and without thinking of Annabel or him or of what had happened in this house. (p.100)

Always there is the awareness of the need to transcend the personal, without denying its importance, allowing it to find its own place. Menzies himself is driven by a vision of Annabel as the light and delight at life's core and through their conversations, through Urquhart's own knowledge of her, this vision is somehow clear to both men. And although Urquhart does not really comprehend its intensity, he is clearly aware of its significance.

> I suddenly saw, then, that the expression on Annabel's face was her farewell to Douglas Menzies on the night of the wreck. The intensity of her love for him was gathered into that moment and, holding it, her ineffable compassion. The smile in her eyes lived as no other light lives. Her hair was disordered and her throat bare.
>
> I was terribly moved, for I knew this was true. Never mind how it came about that I saw it: it was true. And with it came an extra truth, of which at that moment I was equally certain. It was this: within an experience of that kind there are no borders. Love destroys borders.
>
> And long after the event, when the glow dies down and truth withdraws her face, one can still say: anyway, in that experience there is no *fear* of borders. (p.253)

The part played by Annabel is brought closer to Urquhart through his own involvement with the hotel maid, Catherine. This girl, who resembles Annabel Menzies in so many ways, is a constant reminder to Urquhart of the quality which had first struck him on reading Menzies' typescript with its vision of a love that transcended the constraints of the personal. In his own developing relationship with Catherine, Urquhart senses a recurrence of that original love and is aware of something in this recurrence which the mind cannot grasp.

Menzies, however, holds the key. It is he alone who has the capacity to make Urquhart *see* what is before him.

> I saw things more sharply than I had done before. When his eyes followed a fulmar their expression went glimmering deep inside him to such old familiar seascapes as I felt might yet haunt myself. This haunting indeed seemed to be something I already vaguely knew, like that earlier fantastic traffic with the other landscape. The absence of talk instead of inducing a sense of strain completely dissipated it. (p.226)

Following Menzies' gaze, Urquhart catches once again an intimation of the 'other' landscape, the world of light and delight.

> Where the channel ended the dark edges of the cliffs ran with light. A magnificent gateway. Beyond, the sea floor had a golden sheen from the evening sun and extended to a horizon that ran its

fabulously distant line against an ultimate of molten silver. The
sea moved under it and we were suspended. (p.226)

Shortly after this, Menzies tells Urquhart of his own struggle for
understanding. After his wife's funeral he had returned to the
empty house, only to find that this very emptiness brought her
back into his mind. To get away from the pain of this he had
walked to the cliff-edge, from where he had caught sight of a
body in the sea, probably drowned in the storm on the night of
Annabel's death. He decided to go down the cliff, knowing full
well the danger involved.

> He did not expect to be able to go down the cliff and the fatal
> aspect of this knowledge was far in his mind. The desire to get
> away from where he was had grown on him very strongly. If he
> slipped and fell he would be on the way—or at its end. It was the
> way Annabel had gone; there was that for company, anyhow.
> This friendly thought, this warmth in the emptiness, brought all
> his forces together and freed him and he felt nimble. (pp.231–2)

Yet in taking this step into the unknown, Menzies finds that he
has actually hit on traces of an earlier track so that by remaining
calm and collected he is able to follow this and so reach the
bottom. By the time he gets there the body has disappeared,
and all he can salvage is a large cask of rum which he manages
to manoeuvre into a cave. 'He worked away like a man
possessed and occasionally did have bouts of superhuman
strength that came from a terrible drive within him to drive
beyond himself. The cask did not matter.' (pp.232–3)

The next day he returns to this cave at the foot of the cliffs,
and again struggles with the cask, trying to get it into a position
above the water level. In some way this intense physical
activity, wrestling with the heavy cask in the darkness of the
cave, is a way of beginning to come to terms with Annabel's
death.

> It was a slow, cold, wet business, only worth mentioning
> because it produced a bodily discomfort, a misery, that was almost
> pure.
> A curious detachment comes from this misery, a disinterested-
> ness, and at the same time a commingling with sea, rock, slime.

Physical life has reached rock bottom; it has in a mysterious way come home. Something of this can be experienced in daylight, but in darkness, in a cave, there is touch, deliberate conscious touch, a hand grips, even the inside of the head *feels* the near approach of solid mass; while ears hear what is lost in the light and nostrils discriminate a smell into its sources lest there be one dangerous source. It is an elemental traffic which cannot be carried much farther. It generates in time the cold glow of a thin fine delight. (pp.234–5)

What Menzies is describing is his dawning awareness of the nature of the continual interaction of *yin* and *yang*, the manifestations of Tao as it operates among 'the ten thousand things'. Lao Tsu states clearly that 'reversal is the movement of Tao', meaning that when something reaches its extreme it begins to change into its opposite, and Douglas Menzies' discovery of delight in the midst of misery is a personal discovery of the truth of this, in a way that defuses the force of arguments to the contrary. It is also the discovery of a force which lies behind the distinctions of *yin* and *yang*, the energy of the Tao itself.

A new country opened up inside his head at this time. Misery and absorption, exhaustion and the effort that went beyond itself, induced an odd conception of static time within endless distance. When he could do no more and slid to his haunch and lay, the awful silence of the empty house would threaten its invasion and then for a few moments he would be given more than his normal physical strength. Of this he was quite certain. And he tried to make it clear by saying that he was aware of using a force which was there, inherent in the complex of the moment, and not gratuitously or supernaturally conferred upon him from outside. (pp.235–6)

After this account of Menzies' struggle in the cave, and his discovery of light in the midst of darkness, the two men carry on another of their extravagant conversations and Urquhart, despite his obvious belief in Menzies, reveals that he is not yet quite certain about him: 'Sometimes he seemed to me quite illogical and I pulled him up; his words were thickets that obscured the issue so I hauled him back to it. Once or twice, in

fact, I wondered if I had been over-estimating the man.' (p.238)
Yet contact with Menzies leads Urquhart inexorably nearer and
nearer to an understanding of the other landscape. 'Out of his
words something begins to come, something that does not
belong inside my closed circle of ideas, and then, in a moment,
the face is there in his verbal thicket, like the face in the tree of
my boyhood's puzzle picture.' (p.239) Planes of being tilt and
Urquhart suddenly *sees* Annabel as Menzies sees her.

> This face is alive, near, thinner; the cheek bone and the line
> coming down to the chin are smooth and swift. Her hair is in a
> natural disorder as though pushed back by a quick hand. But the
> whole energy of her being is in her eyes. And her eyes recognise
> Menzies with an intensity that is tragic and beautiful . . . I
> perceive there is also compassion in her eyes, as though a woman
> at the end bears all. This terrible living quality, this sheer
> expression of love at its ultimate moment of wordless communion,
> becomes unbearable . . . (p.242)

The vision is too much for him, and he closes his mind to it. It is
only later, when he is talking to Catherine, that he is able to
hold it at a little distance and understand it. Telling her of
Menzies's quest for the Wrecker, he tries to explain his
conviction that Menzies will win through in the end.

> He was bigger than the Wrecker. And what made him bigger was
> love, because love was the creative element, not the wrecking
> element, the creative element that made his music. And that's
> where Annabel came in. For she was part of the creative element
> that made him whole. Without that part, creation is non-human
> and a metaphysical delusion. (p.258)

This aspect of Menzies is best seen when he goes down the
cliff in a storm to rescue Dan Maclellan and a hotel guest who
are in danger of being driven on to the rocks. In the event Dan's
boat is smashed, but Menzies is able to reach the two men and
pull them to safety. Ropes had been brought while Menzies
made his way unaided down the cliff-face, and the men are
hauled up by those waiting on the cliff-tops. The whole episode
recalls Finn's daring exploits in *The Silver Darlings* and also
echoes an incident in *The Key of the Chest*, where the 'outsider'

landlord Michael Sandeman is involved in a cliff rescue and as a result of that incident is integrated with the community which had previously kept itself at a little distance. In *The Other Landscape* it is Menzies who is the outsider, and his selfless action in saving the two men brings him closer to his wife's people.

It also signals the end of Menzies' feelings of guilt about Annabel's death. This encounter with the same sea on the same cliffs, among the same people he had been with on the night of her death brings home to him the inevitability and impersonality of death, and his character begins to lose the distortion caused ! y guilt and to take on its natural shape. And this is the Menzies Urquhart sees on his last visit to the white house. After losing his torch, Urquhart had managed to stumble across the darkness of the moor in the storm to seek out Menzies and arrived at the white house to catch a privileged glimpse of the man at the piano before he realises he is being watched.

> Grandeur, devastation, unbounded force . . . they were the shiver on the skin, blind from achieving nothing . . . In there at the piano was something other . . . I turned my head and looked in. He was playing more slowly, with a curious concentration, as though watching what his hands were doing. I watched, too, and listened, and was beset by that wonder to which there is no end and no key. His head lifted a little. He was not watching his hands, he was listening. And I was caught up in a way I cannot now remember, though I remember, as it were, its country, its climate. My eyes came back to the door where I had seen Annabel. It was closed. Nearer to me was the table with its confusion of papers. White papers were on the floor. A confusion like a bed from which the spirit had risen. (p.297)

This 'curious concentration' is the outer manifestation of Menzies' calm internal strength; a strength that cannot be forced, but which arises spontaneously and naturally with the liberation of the mind. Urquhart, despite his own increased awareness, is still striving for this liberation without quite achieving it. He is still seeking 'answers' on an intellectual level. In the middle of his last conversation with Menzies he challenges him directly and receives, instead of an answer, a further glimpse of an enigma.

He looked at me. And he was silent.

There was a smile in his eyes and the outer corner of his left eyelid quivered very slightly in a critical, understanding humour. The absence of the superior or complacent was complete. He was detached and human and friendly, though friendly is too warm a word for what I felt was strangely anonymous, yet the humour was there and the compelling latent force or reality of the man; it was waiting there, but communication could not be made, and this for some reason affected me in an uncomfortably naked way. I have said that I could never know the man. It went deeper than that; deep as the realisation that none of us can ever, at this point, meet; the awful realisation of the stranger.

But that cannot be borne for more than a moment, except by those who have learned to bear it. (p.303)

Menzies is silent because he knows there are no 'answers' that can be given in the limited terms of the intellect. But this is not an empty cynicism for, while one cannot describe the movement of Tao in words and concepts, it is possible to demonstrate it in one's being. Thus it is said that Lao Tsu sat like a motionless corpse yet 'revealed himself as a dragon'.[12] Menzies' silence, then, can be seen as a positive demonstration of the paradoxical nature of Enlightenment. Urquhart, however, is unable to rid himself of thought, 'that dark inner disease' for long enough to see this. Always he tries to resolve the paradox, and finds himself no nearer the truth.

He had begun to form coherently in my mind and that was something. The two aspects of him, the two nights, were quite different . . .

But always, this night or that, it was the same face, the same man. Different aspects of the one persistent unity; though as I write that it seems too much like an 'explanation', and even my stomach revolts at the word unity. (pp.250–1)

Freedom comes from the ability to live in the heart of the paradox, the ability to perceive the extraordinary and miraculous quality of the most ordinary and mundane action. And this is a way of seeing that comes from an understanding of the changes of *yin* and *yang* and the movement of Tao. Urquhart knows this, but so far knows it only conceptually. Looking at Menzies he

165

has an intuition of how the opposites of *yin* and *yang* lie at the root of everything:

> . . . the bleakness, the loneliness, of the human condition that strips nakedness to the grey bone and is terrifying beyond all further insights of terror. What horror, what tragic meaningless horrors, the Wrecker works on man, from without—and from within.
>
> Against that darkness man has the light, the warmth, the other insight which love has fashioned for him as his sole weapon in the eternal quest. I saw rather than thought this. I thought of Annabel. (p.307)

But it is only after Menzies' death that Urquhart is able to go beyond his conceptual understanding of this and experience it as a reality. Menzies is killed when he once again tries to go down the cliff-face, this time to get some rum from his secret store in the cave for the man he had saved earlier from certain death in the water. Urquhart, who had been with him, is momentarily stunned by Menzies' fall but somehow finds the courage and the strength to go down after him:

> . . . already the feeling of sickness was ebbing and, shedding my coat, I put my feet over.
>
> Normally I am rather uncomfortable with heights and more than once have sworn never to tackle a rock face again. On this occasion that feeling of unease (which can so quickly develop a horrible kind of panic) was completely absent. And the sheer astonishment of this, with the utterly unaccustomed feeling of mastery in it, helped me. (p.310)

Reaching Menzies' body, Urquhart pulls it on to the ledge where Menzies himself had so recently hauled Dan Maclellan. And, realising that when the community discover Menzies' death there will be a lot of empty talk of the drunkard's climb down the cliff for the rum, he decides to get rid of the cask. The cask destroyed, Urquhart returns to Menzies' body, his mind cleansed of bitterness. And the reader is left with the idea of an identification between the two men, Urquhart's cliff-climb and struggle with the cask of rum being a 'recurrence' of crucial episodes in Menzies' own quest. With this identification,

Urquhart comes into his own as an explorer of the other landscape. Assuming the role of Menzies has taken him beyond the personal, beyond the reach of conceptual thought. But the quest does not end here, for in this quest there is no end, only a deepening awareness of the nature of this other landscape. The encounter with Menzies was important not because it supplied 'answers', but because is served as a constant reminder that such 'answers' are incomplete.

> Scraps of the talk came back which we had had in the white house, but in a moment they were like some ogham script, scrawled in stones, about something beyond what could be said, something other. And though nothing of this other might be known, or nothing that could be conveyed, yet equal to it and indeed in some mysterious way going beyond it was the sheer wonder of man's being on its quest. (p.318)

This quest is life itself, and the fact that it has no answer, no end, is what makes it delightful for it is a continuing exploration of an inherently creative process and as such leads to a development of the creativity of each individual: '. . . the self does not become self-centred or egotistic but on the contrary expands into wonder. It apprehends a whole greater than itself, but of which itself is part, and in this apprehension is delight's essence.'[13] The delight comes from the recognition of man's place in the pattern of things:

> Man follows the earth.
> Earth follows heaven.
> Heaven follows Tao.
> Tao follows what is natural.[14]

But this apparent simplicity takes a lifetime to learn. Intellectual understanding is only the very beginning. True understanding comes only when one's every action is carried out effortlessly, in accord with the natural movement of Tao. And often, as in the case of Douglas Menzies, it comes only when one has 'forgotten the words'.

CELEBRATION OF THE LIGHT

This, too, was the case for Neil Gunn himself who published only one other full-length book after *The Other Landscape*, the autobiographical *The Atom of Delight*. And as he told John Pick in the late 1960s, his interest after that moved away from writing to an exploration of the inner world of the spirit, the 'other landscape' itself. Mr Pick recalls the conversation:

> 'When I finished *The Atom of Delight* I felt that was the end of my youth and now I'd really get down to it.'
>
> 'You mean you had made notes for the flight and now you would take off?'
>
> 'That's it. I would start the real work and have a few years for it. But the energy wasn't there. You need to be able to concentrate. And I couldn't manage it. Otherwise I could have gone far enough, I think, where it matters.'[1]

However much ill-health might have robbed him of the necessary energy for this way of life, it was obviously one he found congenial, even achieving a certain mastery as is clear from Professor Hart's description of his first meeting with Gunn.

> After four years of increasingly informal correspondence, I first visited Neil at Dalcraig in the summer of 1965, when he was seventy-four and quite serene and I was thirty-eight and entering nervous academic middle age. Had I taken him at once on his own newly won terms, it might have been easier for us both, but I, alas, came with an academic-historical interest in his career and

his development as a writer, and tended to force him, in his patient kindness, to dredge up the accidentals of which this essay is largely made. He on the other hand was working towards mastery of the peaceful disciplines of concentration and quite able to answer my demands for the cause-effect of literary biography with zen *koans* about wild geese.[2]

Hart's description of this first encounter with Neil Gunn echoes nicely Urquhart's descriptions of his encounters with Menzies in *The Other Landscape* and serves to bring to mind all those similar encounters between the innocent and the wise that are so much a part of his fiction: Aniel and the Master; Elie and Mairi; Young Art and Old Hector.

But the image of Neil Gunn himself as another 'wise old man' is not the whole story. The reality of the man, as his biographers have shown, was much more complex than that. Whatever wisdom Gunn managed to achieve was hard-won and gathered bit by bit over a long life. While most of the later books are literally filled with light, that light is only glimpsed in elusive flashes in the earlier novels.

Yet it is undeniably there. And it is invariably linked to community and environment. Maggie in *The Grey Coast* has her moment of Enlightenment by grasping how she fits in to the elemental world around her, 'the eternal mating of cliff and sea'. And in *The Lost Glen* Ewan Macleod has this marvellous vision of his community.

> From a great distance came back into focus the field of his mind . . . slowly gathering the green of grass, the tumble of the sea; gathering colour and shape, the sweep of a mountain, the bright acres of the crofts. Figures became recognisable; they moved slowly, as if time were a benediction and space the wind-swept playground of thought.
>
> This might be reality extended into the dream, the colours intensified, the humans endowed with wisdom and lit eyes. But its pattern was abiding, its essence true, and its truth desirable.
>
> This had come upon him with a calm and ineffable certainty.
>
> He had known then that it had been at the back of his mind always as an unconscious standard.[3]

Gunn's vision of the light grew naturally out of the traditions of his own people. It was not something *added on* as a comforting solution to the problems faced by that community. Indeed the bitterness and anger of those early books is directly related to Gunn's fear that everything positive and valuable was being drained out of it.

Gunn's fiction, however, does not just preserve but also extends that tradition. Those who see him as being merely a sensitive recorder of Highland life are closing their eyes to the most vital aspect of his art—the constant awareness of 'the other landscape'.

It is here that Gunn connects most clearly with Eastern philosophies: in the idea that there is something more, some other 'real' world beyond the apparent solidity of this world. But Zen, like Gunn, is clear in its insistence that the 'real' world is simply this world seen with renewed vision. The 'other landscape' is not another place: it is another way of seeing. Gunn's background had given him a keen awareness of life as an endless continuum of interrelated events and experiences. His 'discovery' of Zen merely confirmed and helped to expand his own intuitions and insights. It came too late to influence him directly, but the discovery of a philosophical tradition that had for centuries explored areas similar to those he had tentatively explored in his own novels was heartening.

But Neil Gunn was no infallible Zen master. He was a man with human fears and weaknesses just like any other. Through his writing he learned how to deal with those fears and weaknesses better than most and his fiction remains as a remarkable record of the ways in which an individual can master the darkness and grow into light. And the most remarkable thing is that it is all done very lightly. Gunn's best work is never turgid, but always full of movement and grace: 'the thrill of light as you reach it on, say, a mountain ridge. That fine quality of light in which you feel whole, the light that becomes delight and thrills with a sense of freedom.'[4]

The whole of Neil Gunn's fiction is an attempt to evoke an awareness of the light, an attempt to awaken his readers to a sense of life's endless creativity. It is all there in the opening

171

sentence of *Morning Tide*: 'The boy's eyes opened in wonder.' This awareness is simple and natural and irradiated with the wonder that recognises the quick movement of life itself and is able to accept it in its entirety, is able to see that it is *all* a celebration of the light.

LIGHT, DELIGHT AND ZEN

Note: Manuscripts

National Library of Scotland (N.L.S.), Deposit 209, (N. M. Gunn Papers, deposited by J. W. M. Gunn 1973) consists of 33 boxes of miscellaneous printed, typed, and hand-written items. This includes much correspondence, often with drafts of Gunn's replies. Quotations from Dep. 209 are identified in references first by box number and then where applicable, by folder number.

Chapter 1

1. R. H. Blyth, *Haiku* (4 vols., Tokyo, Hokuseido Press, 1949), vol. 1, p.ix
2. F. R. Hart & J. B. Pick, *Neil M. Gunn: A Highland Life* (London, John Murray, 1981), p.242
3. N. W. Ross (ed), *The World of Zen* (London, Collins, 1962). This together with all the other works referred to in this paragraph are listed in the bibliography.
4. N. M. Gunn, letter to F. R. Hart, 11 August 1964. MS, National Library of Scotland, Accession No. 7231
5. J. B. Pick, letter to J. Burns, 28 February 1978
6. N. M. Gunn, letter to F. R. Hart, 11 August 1964. MS, N.L.S., Accession No. 7231
7. N. M. Gunn, letter to Professor T. Nakamura, 26 June 1965. MS, N.L.S., Deposit 209, box 19
8. N. M. Gunn, 'The Flash' in *The Saltire Review*, vol. 5, no. 16 (Autumn 1958), p.23
9. The articles are:
   'The Heron's Legs,' vol. 5, no. 15 (Summer 1958), pp.19–22
   'The Flash,' vol. 5, no. 16 (Autumn 1958), pp.18–23

REFERENCES

'Eight Times Up,' vol. 5, no. 17 (Winter 1958), pp.19–23
'Remember Yourself,' vol. 6, no. 18 (Spring 1959), pp.22–8
'Landscape Inside,' vol. 6, no. 19 (Autumn 1959), pp.43–6
'Highland Space,' vol. 6, no. 23 (Winter 1961), pp.45–8

10. F. R. Hart quoted here from 'Neil M. Gunn: A Brief Memoir' in A. Scott & D. Gifford, *Neil M. Gunn: The Man and the Writer* (Edinburgh, Blackwood, 1973), p.55
11. J. B. Pick, 'The Boy in the Stream' in Scott & Gifford, pp.295–317
12. J. B. Pick, letter to J. Burns, 29 March 1979
13. N. M. Gunn, 'Light' in *Point*, no. 3 (Summer 1968), p.7
14. Chang, Chen-chi, *The Practice of Zen* (London, Rider & Co., 1960), p.147
15. A. W. Watts, *The Way of Zen* (London, Thames & Hudson, 1957), p.88
16. A. W. Watts (with the collaboration of A. Chung-liang Huang), *Tao: The Watercourse Way* (London, Jonathan Cape, 1976), pp.92–3
17. L. Whyte, *The Next Development in Man* quoted here from Watts, *Tao: The Watercourse Way*, pp.112–13
18. S. Suzuki, *Zen Mind, Beginner's Mind* (New York, Weatherhill, 1970), p.21
19. A. W. Watts, *Cloud-Hidden, Whereabouts Unknown* (London, Jonathan Cape, 1974), p.163
20. Watts, *The Way of Zen*, pp.155–6
21. Hsiang-yen, quoted here from Watts, *The Way of Zen*, p.145
22. N. M. Gunn, 'Landscape Inside,' p.46
23. N. M. Gunn, 'The Flash,' p.18
24. Gunn, 'The Flash,' p.19
25. N. M. Gunn, 'Eight Times Up,' p.21
26. N. M. Gunn, 'Light,' p.7
27. Gunn, 'Light,' p.12
28. M. McCulloch, *The Novels of Neil M. Gunn* (Edinburgh, Scottish Academic Press, 1987), p.4

Chapter 2

1. J. C. Cooper, *Taosim: The Way of the Mystic* (Wellingborough, Aquarian Pub. Co., 1972), p.15
2. J. Hamilton-Merritt, *A Meditator's Diary* (London, Souvenir Press, 1976), p.143
3. F. Capra, *The Tao of Physics* (London, Wildwood House, 1975), p.202
4. R. Wilhelm & C. G. Jung, *The I Ching or Book of Changes* (London, Routledge & Kegan Paul, 1975), pp.280–1
5. F. R. Hart quoted here from 'Neil M. Gunn: A Brief Memoir' in Scott & Gifford, *Neil M. Gunn: The Man and the Writer*, p.36
6. M. H. Rescanières quoted here from 'Scottish Saga: Sun Circle and Butcher's Broom' in Scott & Gifford, pp.96–7

7. R. Wilhelm & C. G. Jung, *The Secret of the Golden Flower: A Chinese Book of Life* (London, Kegan Paul & Co., 1931), p.100
8. T. Merton, *The Way of Chuang Tzu* (New York, New Directions, 1969), pp.42–3
9. Wilhelm & Jung, *The I Ching*, p.295
10. Sokei-an Sasaki quoted here from Watts, *The Way of Zen*, p.121
11. C. M. Grieve, *The Complete Poems of Hugh MacDiarmid* (2 vols., London, Martin, Brian & O'Keeffe, 1978), vol. I, p.102

Chapter 3

1. N. M. Gunn, letter to C. M. Grieve, 3 December 1937. MS, N.L.S., Dep. 209, bx. 17, f. 3
2. A. W. Watts, *This is It* (New York, Vintage Books, 1973), p.18
3. Watts, *This is It*, p.19
4. Gia-Fu Feng & J. English (trs), *Lao Tsu: Tao Te Ching* (London, Wildwood House, 1973), ch. 16
5. A. W. Watts, *The Way of Zen*, p.136
6. Chang Chen-chi, *The Practice of Zen* (London, Rider & Co., 1960), p.18
7. Hui-neng, *T'an Ching* quoted here from A. W. Watts, *In My Own Way* (London, Jonathan Cape, 1973), p.192
8. Wilhelm & Jung, *The Secret of the Golden Flower*, p.23
9. Gunn, 'Light,' p.11
10. R. Takashina, Primate of the Soto Zen Sect, quoted here from T. P. Leggett, *The Tiger's Cave* (London, Rider & Co., 1964), p.181
11. D. T. Suzuki, *Essays in Zen Buddhism* (3 vols., London, Luzac & Co., 1927, 1933, 1934), vol. I, p.215
12. N. M. Gunn, letter to Professor T. Nakamura, 26 June 1965. MS, N.L.S., Dep. 209, bx. 19, f. 6
13. Suzuki, *Essays III*, pp.318–19
14. Te-shan translated by R. Sasaki quoted here from Watts, *The Way of Zen*, p.131
15. S. Suzuki, *Zen Mind, Beginner's Mind*, p.102
16. Hui-neng quoted here from D. T. Suzuki, *The Zen Doctrine of No Mind* (London, Rider & Co., 1974), p.55
17. N. M. Gunn, *The Atom of Delight* (London, Faber & Faber, 1956), p.87
18. Suzuki, *Essays I*, p.220
19. Gunn, *The Atom of Delight*, p.241
20. Suzuki, *Essays I*, p.247
21. Gunn, *The Atom of Delight*, p.233

Chapter 4

1. N. M. Gunn, diary, 3 September 1939. MS, N.L.S., Dep. 209, bx. 1, f. 2
2. Gunn, diary, 4 September 1939. MS, N.L.S., Dep. 209, bx. 1, f. 2

3. N. M. Gunn, *Highland River* (Edinburgh, The Porpoise Press, 1937), pp.71–2
4. Gunn, *The Highland River*, p.274
5. *Tao Te Ching*, 25, quoted here from Feng & English
6. N. M. Gunn, 'Highland Space,' p.45
7. Gunn, 'Highland Space,' p.47
8. Scott & Gifford, *Neil M. Gunn: The Man and the Writer*, p.124
9. J. Krishnamurti, *The Wholeness of Life* (London, Gollancz, 1978), pp.141–2
10. For this quotation I am indebted to J. B. Pick who unfortunately cannot recall its source. It appears as the epigraph to Mr Pick's novel *The Fat Valley* (London, Arco Publications, 1959)
11. Gunn, *The Atom of Delight*, p.101
12. Gunn, *The Atom of Delight*, pp.264–5
13. Wilhelm & Jung, *The Secret of the Golden Flower*, p.88
14. Wilhelm & Jung, *The Secret of the Golden Flower*, p.90

Chapter 5

1. E. Muir, 'A "Mature" Book', *The Scots Magazine*, XXXIX, 5 (August 1943), p.382
2. F. R. Hart, *The Scottish Novel* (London, J. Murray, 1978), pp.356–7: 'Two serpents have warred in Tom . . . Tom's sceptical modernity has become a cunning destructiveness, a serpent of intellectual negation. The serpent of wisdom is the counterforce.'
3. A. W. Watts, *The Wisdom of Insecurity* (London, Rider & Co., 1954)
4. Chuang Tsu, XVII, I, quoted here from T. Merton, *The Way of Chuang Tzu* (New York, New Directions, 1969), p.86
5. N. M. Gunn, letter to Iain MacArthur, 8 July 1969. MS, N.L.S., Dep. 209, bx. 11, f. 4
6. N. M. Gunn, diary, 3 September 1939. MS, N.L.S., Dep. 209, bx. 1, f. 2
7. N. M. Gunn, 'A Balance Sheet,' *The Scots Magazine* XXXIV, 4 (January 1941), p.259 (written under the pseudonym Dane McNeil)
8. *Tao Te Ching*, 29, quoted here from Feng & English
9. J. Krishnamurti, *The First and Last Freedom* (London, Gollancz, 1954), p.38
10. Krishnamurti, *The First and Last Freedom*, p.42
11. *Tao Te Ching*, 25, Feng & English
12. H. Wilhelm, *Change: Eight Lectures on the I Ching,* (London, Routledge & Kegan Paul, 1960), p.19
13. G. Bruce quoted here from 'Handling the Unbearable: The Serpent and The Drinking Well' in Scott & Gifford, *Neil M. Gunn: The Man and the Writer*, pp.232–3
14. *Tao Te Ching*, 36, Feng & English
15. *Tao Te Ching*, 52, Feng & English

Chapter 6

1. N. M. Gunn, letter to Geoffrey Faber, 22 October 1950. MS, N.L.S., Dep. 209, bx. 11, f. 5b
2. S. Conn quoted here from 'The Well of Delight' in Scott & Gifford, *Neil M. Gunn: The Man and the Writer*, p.258
3. *Tao Te Ching*, 20, quoted here from Feng & English
4. Watts, *Cloud-Hidden, Whereabouts Unknown*, p.177
5. D. T. Suzuki, *Sengai, The Zen Master* (London, Faber & Faber, 1971), p.7. N.L.S. Dep. 209, bx. 25 contains Gunn's copy of the catalogue of a travelling exhibition of Sengai's work which toured Europe 1961–63. *Sengai the Zen Master* is an expanded version of Suzuki's commentary in this catalogue.
6. E. Wood, *Zen Dictionary* (Harmondsworth, Penguin, 1977), p.57
7. Chogyam Trungpa, *The Myth of Freedom* (Berkeley, Shambhala, 1976), p.156
8. Chuang Tsu quoted here from Gia-Fu Feng & J. English, *Chuang Tsu: Inner Chapters* (London, Wildwood House, 1974), p.159
9. R. H. Blyth, *Zen and the Zen Classics* (New York, Vintage Books, 1978), pp.71–2
10. Watts, *The Way of Zen*, p.27
11. Ch'ing-yuan quoted here from Watts, *The Way of Zen*, p.126

Chapter 7

1. Seng-tsan, *Hsin-hsin Ming* quoted here from Watts, *The Way of Zen*, p.115
2. F. R. Hart, 'The Hunter and the Circle: Neil Gunn's Fiction of Violence', *Studies in Scottish Literature*, 1 (1963–4), p.71
3. J. Krishnamurti, *Beyond Violence* (London, Gollancz, 1973), p.85
4. Krishnamurti, *Beyond Violence*, p.74
5. N. M. Gunn, *The Well at the World's End* (London, Faber & Faber, 1951), p.294

Chapter 8

1. D. T. Suzuki, *The Field of Zen* (London, The Buddhist Society, 1969), pp.5–6
2. Suzuki, *Essays I*, p.290
3. Watts, *The Way of Zen*, p.163
4. Suzuki, *Essays I*, p.266
5. N. M. Gunn, *Butcher's Broom* (Edinburgh, The Porpoise Press, 1934), p.319
6. Suzuki, *Essays I*, p.248
7. Suzuki, *Essays I*, p.155

8. N. M. Gunn, *The Green Isle of the Great Deep* (London, Faber & Faber, 1944), p.246
9. Tao-sheng, quoted here from Chang Chung-yuan, *Creativity and Taoism* (New York, Julian Press, 1963), pp.43–44
10. R. Powell, *Zen and Reality* (London, Allen & Unwin, 1961), p.28
11. J. B. Caird, 'Neil Gunn: The Man and His Art' *The Weekend Scotsman*, 27 September 1975
12. Chang Chung-yuan, *Creativity and Taoism*, p.124
13. N. M. Gunn, *The Atom of Delight*, p.271
14. *Tao Te Ching*, 25, quoted here from Feng & English

Chapter 9

1. Hart & Pick, p.254
2. Scott & Gifford, p.58
3. N. M. Gunn, *The Lost Glen* (Edinburgh, The Porpoise Press, 1932), p.46
4. N. M. Gunn interviewed by George Bruce for the film *Light in the North*. Typescript, N.L.S. Dep. 209, bx. 10, f. 2

GLOSSARY

This brief glossary is intended simply to remind readers of some of the main Zen Buddhist and Taoist ideas which are used in the text. Many of these matters are still being hotly debated by Zen scholars, so there is no attempt here to be exhaustive.

Bodhidharma	The First Patriarch of Zen, who is said to have introduced Buddhism to China from India in the early sixth century BC.
Chuang Tsu	Taoist philosopher who placed great emphasis on *wu-wei*, or not 'forcing' issues.
Dhyāna	Sanskrit word meaning 'meditation'. In Chinese this became 'Ch'an', and in Japanese 'Zen'.
I Ching	*The Book of Changes*, or the *I Ching*, is a systematic attempt to record the changes of the opposites, *yin* and *yang*.
Koan	Question which is intended to push the Zen student beyond logic and force him to respond on the level of *prajnā*, or intuitive insight.
Lao Tsu	Taoist philosopher whose work *Tao Te Ching* powerfully asserts the unknowability of the Tao, the 'Way' of the world.
Mandala	A symbol consisting of a circle with a clearly defined centre which is an archetypal symbol of wholeness and integration.
Prajnā	Direct, intuitive awareness.

179

Rinzai	Japanese Zen sect which places great emphasis on the use of the *koan* as a teaching method.
Sanzen	Formal interview between Zen master and student, in which the student presents an answer to the *koan* on which he has been working.
Satori	A moment of sudden awareness, or enlightenment. For D. T. Suzuki this was the most important aspect of Zen.
Soto	Japanese Zen school which places great emphasis on 'quiet-sitting' as a teaching method.
Tao	The 'Way' of things.
Te	The 'power' or 'virtue' inherent in the nature of the Tao.
Tzu-Jan	The spontaneity and naturalness of the Tao, which has no purpose but simply *is*.
Wu-Hsin	The state of 'no-mind', in which man's sense of a separate ego falls away and he realises he is part of the Tao.
Wu-Wei	Action which is not 'forced', but which is natural and spontaneous.
Yin and *Yang*	The two primordial powers, or energies, whose constant 'interaction' moves the Tao.
Zāzen	Formal seated meditation.

BIBLIOGRAPHY

The following bibliography comprises the first editions of the major prose works of Neil M. Gunn together with all the other sources quoted from in the text.

For a more comprehensive bibliography of the works of Neil Gunn readers are referred to:

Aitken, W. R. 'Neil M. Gunn: A Bibliography' in A. Scott & D. Gifford, *Neil M. Gunn: The Man and the Writer*, Edinburgh, Blackwood, 1973, pp.387–97.

Hart, F. R. & Pick, J. B, 'Selected Bibliography' in *Neil M. Gunn: A Highland Life*, London, Murray, 1981, pp.302–6.

Stokoe C. J. L. *A Bibliography of the Works of Neil M. Gunn*, Aberdeen, Aberdeen University Press, 1987.

I Works by Neil M. Gunn

The Grey Coast, London, Jonathan Cape, 1926.
Hidden Doors [Stories], Edinburgh, The Porpoise Press, 1929.
Morning Tide, Edinburgh, The Porpoise Press, 1930.
The Lost Glen, Edinburgh, The Porpoise Press, 1932.
Sun Circle, Edinburgh, The Porpoise Press, 1933.
Butcher's Broom, Edinburgh, The Porpoise Press, 1934.
Whisky and Scotland: A Practical and Spiritual Survey [Essay], London, Routledge, 1935.
Highland River, Edinburgh, The Porpoise Press, 1937.
Off in a Boat [Essay], London, Faber & Faber, 1938.
Wild Geese Overhead, London, Faber & Faber, 1939.
Second Sight, London, Faber & Faber, 1940.

Works by Neil M. Gunn——

The Silver Darlings, London, Faber & Faber, 1941.

Young Art and Old Hector, London, Faber & Faber, 1942.

Storm and Precipice, and Other Pieces [Selected Extracts], London, Faber & Faber, 1942.

The Serpent, London, Faber & Faber, 1943.

The Green Isle of the Great Deep, London, Faber & Faber, 1944.

The Key of the Chest, London, Faber & Faber, 1945.

The Drinking Well, London, Faber & Faber, 1946.

The Shadow, London, Faber & Faber, 1948.

The Silver Bough, London, Faber & Faber, 1948.

The Lost Chart, London, Faber & Faber, 1949.

Highland Pack [Essays], London, Faber & Faber, 1949.

The White Hour, and Other Stories [Stories], London, Faber & Faber, 1950.

The Well at the World's End, London, Faber & Faber, 1951.

Bloodhunt, London, Faber & Faber, 1952.

The Other Landscape, London, Faber & Faber, 1954.

The Atom of Delight̃f44[Autobiographical], London, Faber & Faber, 1956.

II Articles by Neil M. Gunn quoted from in this book

'The Boat', *The Scots Magazine* XXVIII, 3 (December, 1937), pp.186–94.

'A Balance Sheet', *The Scots Magazine* XXXIV, 4 (January, 1941), pp.258–62. (Written under the pseudonym Dane McNeil.)

'The Heron's Legs', *The Saltire Review* Vol. 5, No. 15 (Summer 1958), pp.19–22.

'The Flash', *The Saltire Review* Vol. 5, No. 16 (Autumn 1958), pp.18–23.

'Eight Times Up', *The Saltire Review* Vol. 5, No. 17 (Winter 1958), pp.19–23.

'Remember Yourself', *The Saltire Review* Vol. 6, No. 18 (Spring 1959), pp.22–8.

'Landscape Inside', *The Saltire Review* Vol. 6, No. 19 (Autumn 1959), pp.43–6.

'Highland Space', *The Saltire Review* Vol. 6, No. 23 (Winter 1961), pp.45–8.

'Light', *Point* No. 3 (Summer 1968), pp.4–12.

III Other Published Sources

Benoit, H. *The Supreme Doctrine*, London, Routledge, 1955.

Blofeld, J. *The Zen Teaching of Huang Po on the Transmission of Mind*, London, Rider & Co., 1958.

Blyth, R. H. *Haiku*, 4 vols., Tokyo, Hokuseido Press, 1949, 1950, 1952.
Zen and The Zen Classics, New York, Vintage Books, 1978.

Other Published Sources——

Caird, J. B. 'Neil Gunn: The Man and his Art', *The Weekend Scotsman*, 27 September 1975.

Capra, F. *The Tao of Physics*, London, Wildwood House, 1975.

Chang, Chen-chi, *The Practice of Zen*, London, Rider & Co., 1960.

Chang, Chung-yuan, *Creativity and Taoism*, New York, Julian Press, 1963.

Chogyam Trungpa, *The Myth of Freedom*, Berkeley, Shambhala, 1976.

Cooper, J. C. *Taoism: The Way of the Mystic*, Wellingborough, Aquarian Pub. Co., 1972.

Feng, Gia-Fu & English, J. (trs.), *Lao Tsu: Tao Te Ching*, London, Wildwood House, 1973.

Chuang Tsu: Inner Chapters, London, Wildwood House, 1974.

Grieve, C. M. (Hugh MacDiarmid) *The Complete Poems of Hugh MacDiarmid*, 2 vols., London, Martin Brian & O'Keeffe, 1978.

Hamilton-Merritt, J. *A Meditator's Diary*, London, Souvenir Press, 1976.

Hart, F. R. 'The Hunter and the Circle: Neil Gunn's Fiction of Violence', *Studies in Scottish Literature*, 1 (1963–4), pp.65–82.

The Scottish Novel, London, John Murray, 1978.

Hart, F. R. & Pick, J. B., *Neil M. Gunn: A Highland Life*, London, John Murray, 1981.

Herrigel, E. *Zen in the Art of Archery*, tr. R.F.C. Hull, London, Routledge, 1953.

The Method of Zen, tr. R.F.C. Hull, London, Routledge and Kegan Paul, 1960.

Krishnamurti, J. *The First and Last Freedom*, London, Gollancz, 1954.

Beyond Violence, London, Gollancz, 1973.

The Wholeness of Life, London, Gollancz, 1978.

Leggett, T. P. *The Tiger's Cave*, London, Rider & Co., 1964.

McCulloch, M. *The Novels of Neil M. Gunn*, Edinburgh, Scottish Academic Press, 1987.

MacDiarmid, H. (see Grieve, C. M.).

Merton, T. *The Way of Chuang Tzu*, New York, New Directions, 1969.

Muir, E. 'A "Mature" Book', *The Scots Magazine* XXXIX, 5 (August 1943), pp.382–4.

Pick, J. B. *The Fat Valley*, London, Arco Publications, 1959 (see also Hart & Pick).

Powell, R. *Zen and Reality*, London, Allen & Unwin, 1961.

Reps, P. *Zen Flesh, Zen Bones*, Harmondsworth, Penguin, 1971.

Ross, N. W. *The World of Zen*, London, Collins, 1962.

Scott, A. & Gifford, D., *Neil M. Gunn: The Man and the Writer*, Edinburgh, Blackwood, 1973.

Suzuki, D. T. *Essays in Zen Buddhism*, 3 vols., London, Luzac & Co., 1927, 1933, 1934.

Suzuki, D. T.——
   The Zen Doctrine of No Mind, London, Rider & Co., 1974.
   The Field of Zen, London, The Buddhist Society, 1969.
   Sengai, the Zen Master, London, Faber & Faber, 1971.
Suzuki, S. *Zen Mind, Beginner's Mind*, New York, Weatherhill, 1970.
Watts, A. W. *The Wisdom of Insecurity*, London, Rider & Co., 1954.
   The Way of Zen, London, Thames & Hudson, 1957.
   This is It, New York, Vintage Books, 1973.
   In My Own Way, London, Jonathan Cape, 1973.
   Cloud-Hidden, Whereabouts Unknown, London, Jonathan Cape, 1974.
   (With the collaboration of A. Chung-liang Huang) *Tao: The Watercourse Way*, London, Jonathan Cape, 1976.
Wilhelm, H. *Change: Eight Lectures on the I Ching*, London, Routledge and Kegan Paul, 1960.
Wilhelm, R., & Jung, C. G. (Tr. Cary F. Baynes) *The Secret of the Golden Flower: A Chinese Book of Life*, London, Kegan Paul & Co., 1931.
   The I Ching or Book of Changes, London, Routledge and Kegan Paul, 1968.
Williams, W. C. *Pictures from Breughel and Other Poems*, Norfolk, Connecticut, New Directions, 1962.
Wood, E. *Zen Dictionary*, Harmondsworth, Pelican, 1977.

INDEX